CW00495548

The Lonely Funeral

The Lonely FUNERAL

Poets at the Gravesides of the Forgotten
Maarten Inghels & F. Starik

Selected by Maarten Inghels,
F. Starik & Stefan Wieczorek

Reports translated by
Jonathan Reeder

Poetry translated by
David Colmer, Donald Gardner, Michele Hutchison,
John Irons, Francis R. Jones & Jonathan Reeder

PUBLICATIONS
2018

Published by Arc Publications
Nanholme Mill, Shaw Wood Road,
Todmorden OL14 6DA, UK
www.arcpublications.co.uk

Text of Antwerp reports by Maarten Inghels
© 2013 Maarten Inghels. Originally published by De Bezige Bij.
Text of Amsterdam reports by F. Starik
© 2005, 2011, Nieuw Amsterdam, Amsterdam.
For all other text, © authors as named.
Translation copyright © David Colmer, Jonathan Reeder
& other translators as named, 2018
Copyright in the present edition © Arc Publications, 2018

Design by Tony Ward
Printed in Great Britain by
TJ International, Padstow, Cornwall

978 1910345 52 8 (pbk)
978 1910345 82 5 (ebk)

Cover design
Tony Ward

ACKNOWLEDGEMENTS
Arc Publications is grateful to De Bezige Bij for permission
to publish selected reports by Maarten Ingels from *De eenzame uit-
vaart* (De Bezige Bij Antwerpen, 2013) and to Nieuw Amsterdam for
permission to publish selected reports by F. Starik from *Een steek diep*
(Nieuw Amsterdam Uitgevers, 2011) and *www.eenzameuitvaart.nl*.
Arc Publications gratefully acknowledges the support of the
Dutch Foundation for Literature (letterenfonds.nl) and Flanders
Literature (flandersliterature.be).

This book is in copyright. Subject to statutory exception
and to provision of relevant collective licensing agreements,
no reproduction of any part of this book may take place without
the written permission of Arc Publications.

Arc Publications Anthologies in Translation Series
Series Editor: Jean Boase-Beier

*Arc Publications would like to dedicate
the English-language edition of this
anthology to the poet and artist
F. Starik
who was one of the key figures in setting
up the 'Lonely Funeral' project in The
Netherlands. For nearly two decades he
worked tirelessly to ensure the project
not only survived but flourished, and
his untimely death in March 2018 has
robbed it of one of its most dedicated
contributors.*

CONTENTS

Foreword / 9

AMSTERDAM FUNERALS

FUNERAL NO.	REPORT	POET	PAGE
0	F. Starik	F. Starik	13
1	F. Starik	F. Starik	15
14	F. Starik	Rogi Wieg	21
18	M. Wigman	Menno Wigman	27
36	F. Starik	Anneke Brassinga	31
37	F. Starik	Judith Herzberg	37
49	F. Starik	Alfred Schaffer	43
55	F. Starik	Maria Barnas	48
57	F. Starik	Erik Lindner	55
67	F. Starik	F. Starik	60
75	F. Starik	Neeltje Maria Min	65
94	F. Starik	Menno Wigman	74
101	F. Starik	Neeltje Maria Min	78
102	F. Starik	Erik Menkveld	83
163	E. Gerlach	Eva Gerlach	89
188	F. Starik	Maria Barnas	94

ANTWERP FUNERALS

11	M. Inghels	Stijn Vranken	101
13	M. Inghels	Maarten Inghels	105
15	M. Inghels	Jan Aelberts	111
20	M. Inghels	Andy Fierens	115
26	M. Inghels	Stijn Franken	122
34	M. Inghels	Bernard Dewulf	126
40	M. Inghels	Andy Fierens	131
43	M. Inghels	Lies Van Gasse	134
47	M. Inghels	Max Temmerman	138

49	M. Inghels	Peter Theunynck	142
51	M. Inghels	Joke van Leeuwen	146
52	M. Inghels	Maarten Inghels	150
56	M. Inghels	Lies Van Gasse	154
57	M. Inghels	Joke van Leeuwen	157
72	M. Inghels	Max Temmerman	160
85	M. Ingehls	Bernard Dewulf	162

Postscript / 164

FOREWORD

You can start a book by thanking people. I would like to name one person in particular, right off the bat. It was Bart F. M. Droog who, upon being appointed poet laureate of Groningen, resolved to attend those funerals where no one else, or else no one, would come. He decided henceforth to palliate, on behalf of the city, the 'lonely funeral' with a poem. A worthy idea, and without hesitation I thought: count me in. Poets now attend lonely funerals in Amsterdam, Antwerp, The Hague, Groningen, Löwen, Rotterdam and Utrecht.

A 'lonely funeral' is taken to be a burial or cremation with no one present except the four pallbearers, one or two civil servants, the cemetery director and the funeral officiant.

In Amsterdam there are approximately fifteen lonely funerals each year: lifelong junkies, solitary seniors, the occasional suicide. Undocumented migrants, drug mules, vagrants, victims of a questionable crime, professional drunkards who toppled into a canal weeks earlier. Most are discovered in their own home, after complaints by neighbours about the stench in the stairwell. Some go to the grave *nomen nescio*, in which case the poet must make do with a few physical features, a terse police report, a presumed country of origin. The poet's task at a lonely funeral is discreet and accommodating: he or she addresses, in the company of the pallbearers and a civil servant, no one in particular. He is not family. He is not a friend by proxy. The poet brings a salutation to someone he never knew, nor ever will know. To someone no one will ever know.

Since beginning this project in November 2002 – for this is what we call it, a 'project' – it has become a routine. Life invariably goes on as I cycle away from the cemetery in my funeral suit, wave in passing to an acquaintance, who I see turn and look, and think: what a natty dresser, that

Starik. Sometimes it hits me the hardest later, like the time we buried a baby who had only lived for a few hours. The image of the funeral officiant carrying the tiny coffin in her arms to Angels' Corner, her dignified posture, her mindful gait – this image will probably stay with me forever.

I want to thank my beloved for those evenings she listened to my stories, caressed my head. Is it possible to weep for the death of someone you never knew? Should you, in fact? The usual journalistic guideline to measure the 'newsworthiness' of fatalities is, I believe, to divide the number of deaths by the distance in kilometres separating them from us. Three thousand Africans equals one elderly lady on my own street. Then I think of that African guy who never made the news. A stowaway on a cargo ship. Upon arrival at the port of Amsterdam they found his body behind the ship's loading doors. His plan had been to hide in the gap between the inner and outer doors, but somehow he got stuck, misjudged the space, did not realize they would fill it with gas to kill tropical insects. He saw a possibility where there was none. The ship had originated in Abidjan, the former capital of Ivory Coast. You picture the hot, dusty wharf, the ships shimmering in the heat, you see a man saunter inconspicuously along the quay toward a ship about to set sail. He is carrying a rucksack with some clothes, medicine and provisions. You see him weigh up the options, break into a crouched run and hurl himself inside. The last door shuts with a rusty smack and a sudden sigh. As news, it's nothing. An African, whose run for the free West failed.

This collection of poems and essays is now for sale: these anonymous deaths have thus become merchandise. You can purchase their story, or lack thereof. The dead do not benefit, they will not be reimbursed.

Nor will their family. Relatives, if there are any, have not made themselves known. With good reason, one may presume. Some kin remain irreconcilable until the bitter end. No longer our business, they say. But sometimes they show up anyway. We once buried a man who had five children by four different women. Three of the five siblings saw one another for the first time at their father's funeral. The other two had met once before, in passing; they gave the other the once-over: so, apparently we're related. All four mothers kept their children away from that one father. And the children, in retrospect, were glad of it. We, the poets, assume he was not a good man. But the first lesson I learned from the senior Social Service functionary, Ger Fritz, was: we do not judge. We pity no one. For us, all that counts is respect for a person's life. Loneliness can be a choice. We don't know exactly what we're doing; the poet speaks in the darkness. We do not know who we are carrying to the grave. We have no grief of our own.

The bottom line is: every human being deserves respect. Respect: this word has, of late, become defiled by people who loudly demand the space in which to vent at their pleasure. This is not the kind of respect we mean. Our respect is different, aloof.

From the very first funeral there was media interest. Television, radio, documentary-makers, all manner of journalists, photographers, Masters students preparing a thesis on this or that, every week it's something. From the outset, too, it was clear that the funeral itself was off limits to film crews or rubberneckers. The poem is written for the deceased and is recited at the graveside. The poets are not play-acting, they do not direct their words, via the lens of a camera, to an imaginary audience.

The poet is there for the deceased. The product is the situation: the poet and the departed. The pallbearers, the officiant, a Social Services functionary. No more than this. That is all. In addition to providing a disquieting picture of our time, whose heartlessness we can all readily sum up, the lonely funeral in particular documents how poets grapple with anonymous death, and in doing so attempt to understand it. In a sense, this book can even be read as an argument for 'useful art', for life-relevant poetry, even if we find that life amidst death. You could call the lonely funeral a long-term artwork, whereby every deceased person writes a new chapter in the big book of oblivion.

You can connect it to just about anything, really. The simultaneity of things. While the bells toll here, elsewhere an alarm sounds, people kiss, or they shout over the telephone, there's always one thing or another. A person is born every second. And every instant, a person dies.

After a while we began numbering the funerals, to keep track. Those numbers have come to belong to the deceased. For this book, Maarten Inghels, Stefan Wieczorek (the translator of the German edition) and I made a selection of the funerals; this book retains the original numbering.

The names of the deceased are either fictionalized (Amsterdam) or given only by their initials (Antwerp). This was necessary. A family member might not appreciate reading by chance that a long-lost uncle had been given a lonely funeral. Uncle has been given a new name. It is not your uncle.

And yet there is still something niggardly about the fact that even in death, these people are denied an existence, relegated to permanent anonymity. Fictionalized, while there is nothing fictional about them. If only there were.

Nameless we come into the world.

F. Starik

Mr. Van Veen

Monday, 18 November 2002, 9:30 a.m.
Nieuwe Oosterbegraafplaats[1]

Mr. Fritz had suggested I first attend one of these lonely funerals, and then see if I was still so keen on that poem idea. Today's the day. A bleak, calm autumn morning. I wear my best suit. Nearly black. Purplish black. Ger Fritz and Ms. Van den Berg from Social Services are already waiting for me. They are nearly obscured, huddled up against the hedge next to the main entrance. I am only just on time: nine twenty-seven. As though they're waiting for me before they can start. We go straight into a small chapel next to the main entrance. So in fact I'm late. Today we alone will pay our respects to Mr. Van Veen, born in 1928. Mr. Fritz had mentioned a sister with whom there was bad blood; she has not come.

We silently take our place in the front row. A simple pine coffin. A floral arrangement with a blank white ribbon. The pungent smell of dead body. The organ plays an excerpt from the *Peer Gynt Suite*, then a movement of a piece I can't place, and 'The Air' by Bach – apparently it is simply called 'The Air', no mention of Bach. We presume the title does not refer to 'air' in the sense of 'atmosphere', but that it is a mysterious Italian reference to a musical genre. 'The Air' resonates from a peculiarly warbling organ, unseen but close by. Then, at the nod of the officiant, the doors open; the pallbearers are poised, and they roll the coffin in a brisk walking pace to its destination. On the way, Fritz points out the graves of

[1] New Eastern Cemetery, Amsterdam

his various other clients. The coffin is lifted off the bier and placed directly onto the nylon straps stretched across the opening of the pit. Heavy work. We are requested to wait off to one side until the preparations are complete.

At the grave there is what they call a 'coffin lowering device': a rectangular steel tubular frame fitted with a system of cables and pulleys, to some extent concealed by the evergreen trim that covers the gap around the edge of the vault. The pulleys guide the steel cables that will lower the coffin. One needs only to activate the mechanism with a handle, and the coffin will automatically, shakily but steadily, make its way into the vault. Which makes you wonder how they get the straps out from under it.

The officiant speaks: 'We lay Mr. Van Veen to rest. Commit his body to the earth's womb.' He observes a minute of silence, which feels like a long time: does he count slowly to sixty in his head, and perhaps lose count halfway? A chilly gust causes my left eye to water. A ruttish blackbird sounds. The button that is supposed to set the automatic device into motion refuses to comply, so one of the pallbearers has to squat down to flick the backup switch. We each toss a spadeful of sand onto the coffin. Fritz scoops a goodly portion for himself. Ms. Van den Berg, at the hands of the officiant, is given a skimpy helping. An equally modest portion leaves my spade.

Back in the coffee room, we all sign the book of condolence. Fritz puts the cards with our names on them in his folder, to go into the archives. Ah, there's the coffee. A young woman tersely asks whether we want milk with it. Fritz explains the odd musical rendition: the organ was still cold, after the weekend. The elderly officiant joins us. Mr. Prins. Pointy nose, slicked-back hair combed over his scalp in strict symmetry. Fritz calls his attention to the presence of Mr. Starik. The officiant approves. 'Nice idea,' he mumbles. No objection there. And from now on I can call Mr. Fritz 'Ger' – and yet we will continue to 'mister' each other. We like that. He expresses his appreciation that I have worn a funeral suit. I wore this suit to a wedding once. I make a mental note to reserve it for funerals. You never know what gets carried around in your clothes. The hubbub of the wedding subsides, makes way for the hush of the grave. We have another coffee. We're rather enjoying ourselves.

I suggest that, ideally, the poet should read his poem between the first and second musical excerpts. The coffin is already being wheeled out during the third. Fritz thinks first of outside, at the grave, but reconsiders, because that's the officiant's turn to speak, the part about the earth's womb and committing: that's nice, it's enough. No need to add to it.

Let's give it a try, says Ger Fritz. Come to St. Barbara Cemetery this Wednesday at nine thirty, and you'll encounter an unknown man, found dead in an empty flat. No name, no nationality. You'll recite your poem, Mr. Starik. We'll take it from there. 'Have you got anything in hand?' he asks, and: 'How long is it, you know, one of these poems?' I estimate fourteen lines, we'll go for a sonnet. Fritz nods in approval.

I take my time cycling home. On the way I stop to jot down (with the new pen embossed with the name of the funeral collective, a kind of business gift from Mr. Fritz) a few loose lines on the corner of a newspaper. At home I hang the former wedding suit neatly on a hanger.

Monday glides past in a nameless sonnet, which should sound sympathetic yet sensible. What does one say about nobody? A young man, probably from Ghana or Ivory Coast, found in a flat in a suburb of Amsterdam that had apparently sheltered a number of persons and was abandoned in great haste. One presumes these were undocumented persons residing here illegally. Not people, 'persons'. Undesirable aliens. One less.

Name Unknown

*Wednesday, 20 November 2002, 9:30 a.m.
St. Barbara Cemetery
Duty poet: F. Starik*

A pale, vague sun. Mindful of my experience at the Nieuwe Ooster, I'm fifteen minutes early today, but Mr. Fritz is already there. I shake hands with Mr. Degenkamp, director of St. Barbara, who I remember, firstly, from the poet Paul van der Steen's funeral, and later, when we picked out an inexpensive secondhand stone to make into a modest memorial for Paul's grave; it would be ground smooth and have the new name etched onto it. Belgian bluestone, it's called. It is commonly used for entrance steps on the more chic canal houses. Of all the varieties of hard limestone it is the cheapest, and wholly suited to gravestones. I recall with a smile an excerpt by Nescio, in which he describes a group of friends, one of whom, Hoyer, 'would never sit on a blue stoop, because it drew such a chill.'[2] Hoyer was right. The stone draws cold up. Maybe that is what makes it so suitable for the topstone of a grave.

At precisely half past nine the hearse pulls into the cemetery, followed by two passenger cars, from which a total of sixteen men alight. 'See what I mean?' says Mr. Fritz. 'Our friend has a name after all. But what it is, we'll never find out.' 'Now what?' I ask. 'We go ahead as planned,' Fritz says. The men crowd into the reception room. A small man pushes to the fore. 'Muslim,' he says. 'No coffee! Ramadan!'

'We have a speaker,' Fritz says to him. 'There is music,

---

[2] "omdatti daar zoo koud van werd." (Buiten-IJ, 1914)

and then it's the turn of you gentlemen.' So today we will pay our last respects to a dead man, anonymous but at least not alone. He was found in an apartment in the Bijlmer, a social-housing district on the outskirts of Amsterdam. The apartment appeared to have been abandoned in great haste. The deceased had to be found, so the living fled. A young man in his prime, judging from the friends in the prime of their lives, who have come to bid him farewell. Probably from Ghana or Ivory Coast. The Dark Continent.

The coffin is wheeled into the chapel. Music – the generic, everyday Classic FM sort – hesitantly emerges from the sound system. A mobile telephone rings. The group of men has grown to twenty. They enter the chapel, where we are already seated. I have taken off my overcoat, so as to recite my poem without it. There is something so hasty about speaking with your coat still on. The overcoat is new. I bought the long pearl-grey overcoat to complement the almost-black suit. They go well together. Fritz indignantly dismisses my suggestion, in light of the situation, to skip my poem. The group's diminutive foreman enters into a discussion with the officiant, although she does not understand what the discussion is about. It'll be the music, I suppose, but I don't get involved. Another mobile phone rings. Fritz takes the bull by the horns, marching energetically up to the centre of the palaver and saying, in English: 'In or out!' He gestures broadly with his arms. Their foreman points towards the door. The men retreat into the coffee room. The ones who were already seated appear to hesitate. In the end, just one of the men, a youth in fact, decides to stay put. He stays bravely behind, all on his own.

Slow fade-out of Classic FM. The officiant nods. I take my sheet of paper and walk to the lectern. As I speak, I look by turns at the simple wooden coffin, the officiant, Mr. Fritz and the black youth. At the back of the chapel, the pallbearers doze.

* * *

Goodbye, nameless man, I salute you as you pass
into the last of lands where all are welcome,
where no one needs to know a thing about you.
Goodbye, man with no papers, no identity.

What brought you here? Who looks out through an empty
      window
now for you, nameless man, who's waiting as I speak,
as I repeat my empty words in an almost empty room?
I came too late. I never knew you.

Not in your weakness, not in your strength.
Not in the last of lands, where the nameless too are wel-
      come.
I don't even know which language you once spoke.

Who loved you? In which rooms did you sleep?
Who straightened out your sheets and who will wear your
      shirts?
Who will stand in your shoes?
Who will turn down your road?

Who seeks you yet? Who listens for your footfall?
Who heard the voice that lured you
to Amsterdam, your final port of call?

                    F. Starik, translated by David Colmer

    Classic FM is switched back on. The doors open, the
coffin is wheeled outside and we are rejoined by the men
from the coffee room. Yet more men come walking up; I
gesture matter-of-factly for them to join in, too. I am already

getting comfortable in my role as deputy officiant.

The men crowd around the grave. A prayer is recited. They spread their hands, palms turned upwards, make a symbolic face-washing gesture, and mumble along with the refrain. The coffin is lowered. We stare, fascinated, at the free-spinning handle which, at a pinch, can be used to lower the coffin manually. Then the ceremony is over. We shake hands with all twenty-four men. 'Hey,' I say, twenty-four times. 'Thanks,' the men mumble, twenty-four times.

'Okay, so now we have five different names,' the upbeat officiant says as we amble to the coffee room. 'Oh well,' Fritz sighs. 'Twenty-four illegals. Ivory Coast, Ghana, Bijlmer. They suddenly showed up at the funeral home this morning, performed a ritual washing. Decent, yeah?'

'But how could they have known where and when they needed to be?' I ask. 'There's bound to be a grapevine,' Fritz answers diplomatically. 'No crime in that.' There is no police presence today. Sometimes there is, though, in a case like this, on the quiet. Just to keep an eye open. Maybe they'll pick up a name. You don't go arresting somebody at a funeral. 'The small one,' Fritz says, pointing to the foreman, 'is probably running a pop-up mosque in some parking garage. He'll have his contacts. Anyway, they managed to keep it nice and quiet.' He shrugs. 'You'll never find out anyway.'

The officiant compliments me on my poem and the subtlety of the delivery. I was afraid it might come across as high-falutin, but it didn't. 'Who loved you?' she quotes. 'That was really moving. Also the part about the shoes.' Mr. Degenkamp is satisfied too. He thought it was beautiful. Oh well, I say modestly, it's my profession. Degenkamp says he'd like to re-read the text of the poem later, and points to his hearing aid. So he thought something he didn't hear was beautiful. I suppose it was the relief that it all went smoothly. Mr. Fritz would like a copy too, for the archives. He'll file the poem in the dossier of the man with no name. Maybe someday a family member will come asking for the papers. You never know. I changed a word here and there this morning, but that's all right. No, really, he assures me, no problem. 'Well, there you are,' Fritz says as a goodbye, 'the professionals gave you the thumbs up. We'll see how things go from here.' He offers me a warm, damp hand. We'll see how it goes from here. Savouring those words, I cycle slowly homeward.

Name Unknown

Friday, 14 November 2003, 10:30 a.m.
Nieuwe Oosterbegraafplaats
Duty poet: Rogi Wieg

A watery sun. I arrive just after ten, and see Fritz at the entrance in the company of old Mr. Prins, my favourite officiant. Shortly thereafter, we see two police investigators we've met once before, at the funeral of an unidentified woman. That was in December 2002, Rogi Wieg's first lonely funeral. On that occasion the more outgoing of the two, the flamboyant Surinamer with the hat, told us about a friend of his, now deceased, who was an artist and wrote fine poetry. We greet one another as long-lost family. I now know the detective's name is Bruning. Straight away, he continues his story, picking up where he left off months ago. Says he's still planning to send me the collection, 'for sure'. Can't remember if he still has my address. Just a sec, he says. He takes down my address once again, writing in tiny letters on the corner of an envelope. With a flourish, the envelope gets tucked back in his inside jacket pocket. They are here because the man we are going to bury this morning had jumped in front of an oncoming metro train at Reigerbos station. That is their district.

'Man, between twenty-five and thirty years of age, medium skin tone, struck by an oncoming train on 6 November 2003,' he reads from his official report. Then Rogi Wieg arrives, accompanied by Judith Flier, his wife. Is that okay, they ask. By all means. Wieg is wearing a black hat and a long green raincoat. He admits that this is hard for him, in light of his own background, dedicating a poem to the unknown man we are about to lay to rest. Which is why he has brought along his beloved.

When I contacted him earlier this week with the request, I cautiously inquired whether he could handle it. For many years now, periods of profound depression had brought him to psychiatric clinics in the Netherlands and Germany; he underwent electroshock therapy, and subsequently struggled with post-traumatic stress disorder that, understandably, followed his traumatic experiences. 'Only after the depression had thrust itself into my arms did I realize it was Lucifer himself who had nestled there, that he had me in his grip, lifted me off the ground and began squeezing me. Then came the "snap" in my head. The pain came, and with the pain the void, and with the void the pain.' It is a miracle he survived. But he did survive, and answered wholeheartedly yes. 'Especially with my background.'

In the small chapel, a tremulous organ starts up a rendition of a pop ballad. Silent snippets of the lyrics waft involuntarily through my head: *loneliness* and *always* and *love you*. Once the music is finished, Mr. Prins steps forward and says that we are here to pay our last respects to this unknown person, and he invites Mr. Flier to present his poem to the deceased. Wieg walks up front, and, facing the coffin and his back to the small gathering, tells the dead man that he also tried to take his own life. 'I didn't succeed.'[3]

[3] In the end, Wieg did succeed. Unbearable psychological and physical suffering led him to opt for euthanasia, and he died on 15 July, 2015, aged 52.

LEAVE IT AT THAT

Just some of your remains
at this funeral, just some flowers
and a pauper's poet, yes, me.
I too have tried, just not
in front of a train, differently,
less fatally too, I guess, with final seconds
where there might still be time, that's how I tried.

I'm talking to what's left of you,
what they could find, as if to a man
at a station, in a coffee house, what I say
is about the end and that is so ordinary,
so deadly dull it almost makes me blush,
but what is there to say about a drama?
A drama with flowers, no actors.
No characters? For me this is all
just a story: like all of reality.

Rest. Don't do anything else, especially nothing crazy.
Leave it at that and otherwise nature
will probably leave you to it.

Rogi Wieg, translated by David Colmer

It's extremely quiet now. Wieg has laid his poem on top of the coffin. One of the detectives walks forward and takes a photograph – *flash* – first of the coffin, then of our small group – *flash* – and once more: *flash*. Somehow the brief bursts of light deepen the silence. They put the moment of leave-taking on record. Now that we've been photographed together we are a kind of family, on our plain chairs in the small chapel. What, if anything, we hope to prove, I don't know. But it will look good in the archive.

We hear a soft click from the control panel. A lamp will probably go on somewhere. Or a buzzer sounds. Mr. Prins has given the signal to the unseen organist that he can let loose again. There are lots of buttons on the control panel, two of which in particular stand out. Above them is a small sign with the text: CREMATION / BURIAL. The organ enters, this time with a potpourri of suitable classical melodies. As the third musical set begins – again, a popular ballad whose lyrics will lodge themselves in your head, and remain there for a very long time – the doors leading outside swing open. The pallbearers are ready. The circular revolving door holding the coffin looks as though the coffin could also be lowered down through the floor. So the right choice was made for the right button. Before we go outside, Fritz takes Mr. Prins by the arm and gently reminds him that the poet's name is Wieg, not Flier. He winks at me, as though to say: always keep things on a tight leash.

It's quite a walk. Perhaps the wind is slightly chillier than this morning, but it is dry, at least. When we arrive at the grave, Mr. Prins encourages us to gather closer, to form a circle of human warmth: we do it, we're suddenly standing shoulder to shoulder. In the circle of human warmth, we shiver silently as one. I forget to count off the minute's silence with Mr. Prins. I wonder if he actually counts. He is standing there so alone: as officiant, he has kept himself outside our circle. This makes the circle even tighter, and his small figure even more fragile. We silently look one another in the eyes for a while. A chilly gust almost blows the poem from the coffin. That is the sign to end the moment of silence.

Prins whispers, 'Let's do the flowers too this time.' Then the coffin descends into the pit, the flowers lying on top. As a rule, the floral arrangement gets placed at the edge of the grave, among the familiar evergreen branches. A heavy lid lies alongside the grave. This grave cut more resembles a vault, as though its walls are plastered. Usually the cut is shored up by wooden planks, so it doesn't cave in if mourners stand close to the edge. No shovelful of sand this time. There is no shovel. The Nieuwe Ooster is not Catholic. Here, you have to ask for a shovel in advance, as an extra service. And no one asked. We walk slowly back. The Surinam woman whose job it is to guide us through the cemetery takes a different route than on the way here. Was it my imagination, I ask her, or was that grave lined with stone. Yes, she says, it's a burial vault. Slows down the process of decomposition. You can always get out. The cover will soon be placed loosely over the opening. Apparently they reckon that someone will eventually come to collect our unknown person. That this is not yet his final resting place.

Mr. Prins walks beside me. He tells me about the old days. Back in the day, strapping men would dig the grave, nice and straight, they would scoop out a perfect rectangle in the earth. Gravedigging was a craft. Nowadays the cut is dug by a small back-hoe. With the right equipment, now anyone can call himself a gravedigger. Back then there was no electric lift either, so the coffin always had to be lowered on ropes. Still happens now and again. The pallbearers stand right up close to the edge and lean over to ensure the coffin stays level. Hard work. And then a straight-cut grave is essential, so the walls don't collapse. 'I've fallen in before,' Mr. Prins says. 'That was no fun.' 'It makes sense,' I say, trying to reason away my laugh, 'that as the smallest and lightest pallbearer, you'd fall in first.'

We linger in the coffee room for quite some time. The detectives express their admiration for Rogi's poem, and praise our initiative. Mr. Bruning brings up his late friend the artist again, who had produced such wonderful things, and once more he asks for my address. Because he really wants to send me that book. 'It's got wisdom,' he says, 'wisdom about life.' 'Do,' I say. Now Mr. Prins also writes down his address on a slip of paper, because there aren't enough copies of the poem for everyone, and no one at the Nieuwe Ooster can manage the photocopy machine. He would also like a copy of Simon Vinkenoog's poem – remember? he asks – Vinkenoog had been the duty poet at his last lonely funeral, and he didn't dare bring it up. 'Gosh, that man can really knock together a poem,' he pronounces, satisfied. I've heard Mr. Degenkamp say the exact same thing. It sounds artisanal, like physical labour. 'Where's the spade? I'm going to shovel me a poem.'

We take our time saying our goodbyes. Prins takes Judith Flier to one side, and says earnestly: 'Don't worry yourself, now. You know what you should do? When you're lying in bed at night, and you lie there thinking about stuff, then say to yourself: I turn my thoughts over to my subconscious. That's why you've been given a subconscious. And when you wake up the next morning, everything's in apple-pie order.'

Mrs. Put

Wednesday, 31 December 2003, 10 a.m.
Vredenhof Cemetery
Duty poet and report: Menno Wigman

Mrs. Put's lonely funeral was, so to speak, put on ice until after Christmas. So this time I had, rather than three days, a whole week to write a poem. Seven drab days, the last days of December, with the prospect, on the thirty-first at ten in the morning, of covering up the 83-year-old Mrs. Put with a poem.

Mrs. Put had one daughter. Whether she would show up that day was uncertain. In 1957 Mrs. Put divorced her husband. She saw the light of day in 1920, and in 2003 the light went out in St. Lucas Hospital.

As the Christmas holidays progressed, her funeral increasingly began to bother me. That symbolic date, the early hour, it all felt so cheap. What could be more degrading than to be buried on a day when the rest of the world is joyfully heralding a new year? Mrs. Put's death had, in fact, already expired. It depressed me.

But it helped to know that fellow poet Neeltje Maria Min would be reciting a poem on the same day, a half hour after me, at the Nieuwe Ooster. For Mrs. Troost.

They showed clips on TV of the "smoker's poles" on windswept railway platforms. Endangered smokers said their piece. Some dropped the keyword 'America'. From the first of January, everything would be different. Not for Mrs. Put or Mrs. Troost. (Put and Troost – Funk and Comfort – their very names are a gift to a poet.)

I hear the occasional burst of fireworks as I cycle out to

27

Vredenhof on the last day of December. Especially here in the blue-collar Staatsliedenbuurt, they're at it early. The flower stall at the entrance to Vredenhof is doing a roaring trade. This is a day for commemorating all kinds of things.

In the reception room I'm greeted by functionary Ton van Bokhoven. Starik is taking a break abroad. Mrs. Put's daughter is not here.

'Mind if I smoke?' Van Bokhoven asks tentatively. But as a civil servant he knows better than anyone that he's legally got one more day to smoke at a funeral home. After that, smoking is outlawed here too.

The officiant arrives. Once inside, the sound system plays Liszt's *Liebestraum*. For the umpteenth time this week, Rilke's words resound in my head: 'The old woman upstairs with the hacking cough / Yes, she's dead.' As though this coffin, too, doesn't hold a whole life full of love, pain and bruised dreams.

After the Liszt, I read out my poem. Since it's a pretty harsh poem, especially halfway through, I stumble over the words a few times. I almost get the feeling I'm violating a code of conduct. But indeed, this 'embarrassed dragging of feet', as I call it somewhere in my poem, does not feel much like a funeral.

BESIDE MRS P.'S COUNCIL COFFIN

Is she asleep? She is. After eighty-three years
   of combing her hair three hundred and sixty-five
days a year, of walking to the shops and back
   in I don't know how many pairs of shoes,
and all those pairs of laces, the forks, the spoons,
   the people, what people, where, she is asleep.

Asleep and I, morbid as I am, can't help
   but think about her comb, her clippers and eyebrow pencil,
how everything, her lotion, her bank card, her entire era,
   has all been thrown away, erased. And this,
is this embarrassed dragging of feet a funeral?
   As if a coin has slipped unnoticed from your pocket,

or you've forgotten your paper at a bored bus stop.
   That's what it's like. Call it tragedy, rhythm, rhyme –
time, that dirty carnivore, ensures an end
   that stinks. But she's asleep at last, asleep.
So cover her up, make sure her weary feet
   don't need to tread the streets again.

Menno Wigman, translated by David Colmer

Two more pieces of music – why always those safe,
spineless synthesizer tunes?—and then the curtains to the
cemetery slowly open. For moment, it looks like one of the
pallbearers is sneaking a cigarette at the back. But it's just
his breath condensing in the icy morning air.

Back in the coffee room, Ton van Bokhoven tells us that
Mrs. Put had not one, but nine children. Most of them
could not be reached. Two, maybe three, of her children
might have changed their surname. The only daughter they
managed to trace straight away was mentally disabled. She
was born in 1958, a year after her mother's divorce. For her,
as for us, Mrs. Put was a stranger.

Outside, a crescendo of fireworks. As Ton and I stub out
our last cigarette, the coffee lady comments that these will
probably be the very last cigarettes smoked here. There's
just one more funeral after us, and then that will be that.

On my way home I watch the postal rescue workers go
from house to house. Everyone is shopping for things to

see the old year out. On the Kinkerstraat, I pass a beaming mother with three exuberant children. Oh, Mrs. Put, whatever went wrong?

Klara Reina van Metteren

Tuesday 18 January 2005, 10:30 a.m.
Nieuwe Oosterbegraafplaats
Duty poet: Anneke Brassinga

Contrary to every weather forecast, I arrive dry. For the first time since 2 November last year I cycle down the Middenweg, where Theo van Gogh was murdered. There are two parked cars, there's nothing to see, but still one shudders.[4] Anneke Brassinga arrives, far sprucer than on the cover of that volume of hers I have on my bookshelf. Somewhat more up-to-date spectacles than the enormous ones that bedeck her face on the book. She has put on bright red lipstick. She is wearing a synthetic, and therefore completely moth-proof, fur coat.

Mrs. Klara Reina van Metteren was born on 20 April 1941 in Amsterdam and passed away at one in the morning on 7 January 2005 in Onze Lieve Vrouwe Hospital, also in Amsterdam. Her mother died on 14 October 2004 at the age of 101 and was likewise buried at the Nieuwe Ooster. Mrs. van Metteren lived in Portugal for a while; she had a Portuguese husband, but they had been separated for some time. (Her closest relative, an older cousin, does not live in Amsterdam and is unable to attend the funeral.) She was a nurse by profession. She lived in a sturdily-built apartment, with a wall unit and a grandfather clock. In contrast to this domestic orderliness, Social Services encountered utter

---

[4] Theo van Gogh (1957-2004) was a controversial Dutch filmmaker and author, who was brutally murdered by a Dutch-Muslim extremist in broad daylight.

chaos, most likely due to psychological problems.

This is Anneke Brassinga's first lonely funeral. In the run-up, many questions remained unanswered: what did she die of? How long had she been hospitalized? Anneke tries the hospital and gets a pastor on the line who is not prepared to divulge any information, with or without the permission of Mr. Frits. 'I just called him Mr. Frits,' Anneke says, 'because I didn't know his surname.' When I telephone her on Monday evening, she is in the middle of typing the third neat copy of her poem, so as to meet the minimum number of required copies. I explain that it's Mr. Fritz, with a 'z', Ger Fritz. I enquire whether she has a computer, on which she can simply enter the number of desired copies. No, she doesn't have a computer. But has she ever heard of a copy centre? Yes, she's heard of that. 'I know the melancholy of copy centres, of hollow men with yellowed papers, bespectacled mothers with new addresses, the smell of letters, of old bank statements, of income tax returns and tenancy agreements, demeaning ink that says that we exist,' she quotes flawlessly from Menno Wigman's poem 'In Conclusion'. 'And I have seen new suburbs, fresh and dead,' I pick up where she left off, 'where people do their best to seem like people, the street a fair impression of a street.'[5] I wish her luck with the typing. I look forward to the next morning, when I'll be handed a sheet of paper onto which the letters have been hammered, every last one, by the poet herself.

Up walks Ger Fritz. On his day off. He's come anyway. Fritz tells us he has signed his retirement papers. There's no turning back now. And what do you know, there is some family after all: a nearly-deaf uncle, and a second cousin with his wife. We all introduce ourselves, and say why we are here. A person doesn't just show up at a random funeral,

---

[5] English translation of Menno Wigman's 'Tot besluit': David Colmer.

32

there has to be a reason for attending. The small family is appreciative about the presence of a poet. Decent, they say. A fine gesture. The uncle announces that he wishes to recite the Lord's Prayer, as he did at the recent funeral of Mrs. Van Metteren's mother. Agreed. Brassinga will speak between the first and second piece of music, and uncle between the second and third. We begin. Fritz leads us into the chapel, laying a fatherly hand on the shoulder of each person as they enter.

The organist plays an extremely simplified version of 'The Air', then Brassinga speaks, clearly, not too fast, somewhat louder than usual, keeping uncle in mind.

THE CHILD

There is a mother in our life, she is
the ground and knows why we were born,
she everywhere walks on ahead where we
ourselves as yet were still unable – even
on the untrodden soil down in the underworld
though she was laid to rest there, though she
has lived to be a hundred, became almost our child.

You follow her as if she has called out:
Klara, daughter, come, you're sorely missed.
Had you no neighbour or no pet to talk with?
The longcase clock struck every quarter, clank-
clattering refrain of silence. Twelve weeks
you've been an orphan – twelve centuries?
Rest now in peace, be ever reunited.

Anneke Brassinga, translated by John Irons

33

The organist enters with the second number, Vivaldi's 'Autumn'. Uncle takes his place behind the lectern and announces his prayer. He thanks those attending this intimate gathering for being here, and recites the Lord's Prayer without a hitch. 'Our Father in heaven, hallowed be your name, your kingdom come, your will be done, on earth as in heaven. Give us today our daily bread. Forgive us our sins, as we forgive those who sin against us. Lead us not into temptation, but deliver us from evil.' Amen. It is truly a perfect poem. It asks everything that we could, or should, ask of ourselves – call it our conscience – of our situation, and of God. And it pictures God as an enormous father figure, the kindest, the greatest father. Our father. We shall see him. Through me sings: what a beautiful text.

They say Jesus thought up this prayer himself, when his disciples beseeched him, 'Lord, teach us to pray.' He gave them this poem, this call to humility, to forgiveness: the first Christian prayer. The gospel of Luke teaches us that when we pray, we should do so with as little verbal ceremony as possible. We must not presume we can persuade the Almighty to give ear to our plea simply by using a lot of words. Moreover: He has heard us even before we ask Him. He knows full well what we need. The ideal poem, therefore, is a short poem. Because the ideal poem has the effect of a prayer. I think this as the third piece of music begins, the doors swing open and a brilliant, low burst of sun fills the chapel. We stand, but we have to wait our turn: another procession emerges from the large chapel, at least fifty people. Large trumps small. Many before few. The third number is long finished by the time we can finally move on. The organist makes an unsolicited attempt at variations on the theme of the last number, but in the end the music peters out.

Outside, light-green ring-necked parakeets twitter. We have to stop halfway while the other group's coffin is offloaded. As we pass we hear their own pastor recite, once more and from a distance, the Lord's Prayer. I silently mumble the words along with him. We never learned to pray at home, so I had to pick up the Lord's Prayer from friends when I stayed for supper. The steaming dishes on the table. Mother taking her seat, removing her apron. Father glancing solemnly around the table, asking for a moment of silence and crossing himself. You were supposed to shut your eyes. This was difficult. We, the children, would peek at one another through nearly-closed eyelids and attempt to sabotage the prayer by making silent, silly faces, while Mother and Father peeked through their eyelids for potential civil disturbances. And then Father would rattle off the prayer, almost unintelligibly, as though it was an exercise in speed-talking, the World Cup of prayer-mumbling. He would then make a hasty cross. I remember my grandfather making a really small cross, more like tapping his breastbone with his finger, while others would gesticulate with broad swipes of the arm, far from their body, finally touching their shoulders, their head, their belly. My favourite part was the moment after all this, when we could open our eyes again, and there was a short pause before life resumed. In Jerusalem they built a church on the spot where Jesus is said to have taught His disciples the Lord's Prayer. They asked Him a question, twenty centuries ago—'Lord, teach us to pray'—and we still remember the answer.

We wait until the large family's pastor has finished his prayer before continuing. He doesn't exactly rattle it off. I see the family members doing their best to recite the text along with him, you see their lips move the way athletes sometimes fake their way through the national anthem before an important match. You can tell from their lips that they don't know the words. We give the other procession a wide berth on our way to our own grave. Now their large circle has a full view of our modest gathering, as we stand silently alongside the coffin. Moments later we hear a child start to cry. The coffin is lowered. The other family departs. We wait until they are more or less out of sight.

We amble back. To the municipal coffee. Anneke Brassinga tells us how she found the words she was looking for. She went for a long walk, and on the way she looked at random passers-by and thought: who'll be standing alongside your coffin, one of these days? We are in agreement that it takes exactly three days to produce one of these poems. Three days and one sleepless night.

The family drinks one cup of coffee each, fills us in on the history of Klara van Metteren. She had a child, and it died, long ago. Right around then, things must have gone wrong. She never got over it. With much ceremony we say goodbye to the family. We stay behind. Drink more coffee. The pot has to be emptied.

I cycle homeward. By the time I've reached the end of the Middenweg, I have lost my freshly-found faith.

Maria Petronella van Kempen-de Wildt

Monday 28 February 2005, 10:30 a.m.
Nieuwe Oosterbegraafplaats
Duty poet: Judith Herzberg

An improbably clear winter's day. At a quarter past ten I cycle onto the cemetery grounds. I have delivered my son, in the dry, freezing cold, to his school in Amsterdam-West. His hands are chilled to the bone; I rub them warm, and stand in the schoolyard in my good suit chatting with one of the mothers. Under the suit I'm wearing my new long underwear, made of dark-blue synthetic fabric; according to the label it is manufactured using astronautic technology. On the way to the Nieuwe Ooster I stop for an extended coffee in a modern locale where the coffee is treated as a delicacy. Bring it on. Another 62 roasts to go.

Fritz, Mrs. Herzberg, and the officiant stand shivering at the gate. I recall Judith Herzberg with raven-black locks. Now her hair is completely grey. Right away, I make a quip about it. Her repartee: there's more of mine on my photo than in reality. The hearse pulls up, the gravel crunching under its tyres.

For Mr. Fritz, it is his last funeral: this is his final work week before he retires. For Social Services, this is the sixty-seventh funeral to be organized this year. For Judith Herzberg, it is the first she is attending. She will have to make do with these details: Maria Petronella van Kempen-de Wildt had no family: she was an only child, both parents are deceased, widow, no children. She was born on 20 July 1918 in Amsterdam, and was found in her home on 12 February 2005. The only sign of a social network was a

Christmas card postmarked Lelystad.

Social Services informed the Christmas card's sender of the funeral. In the days preceding the funeral I spoke with Herzberg at length by telephone. She wanted to know what was written in the Christmas card. I phoned the office and was told that the card was no longer in the dossier, only an empty green envelope which presumably once contained a Christmas card, judging from the holiday postage stamp and the return address in Lelystad. Meanwhile, the sender has responded: they are unable to be physically present at the funeral, but certainly will be in spirit.

On the Thursday before the cremation, Social Services placed a death announcement in *De Telegraaf* in the hope that someone might still react. I buy a copy of *De Telegraaf* three days running, hoping to locate the announcement, but I can't find it. And Judith Herzberg says that's going too far, buying the newspaper just for that. Then you're stuck with that paper.

We go into the chilly coffee room. A little while later a well-dressed older woman carrying a bunch of white tulips hesitantly enters. Asks if she's in the right place. She is. She introduces herself as a friend. *The* friend, you could say. There was a distant family member in Amsterdam-North too, with whom Maria was not all that close. Aside from that, no, there was indeed no one.

Maria used to play tennis with the woman's husband. Well, you know how it goes. The husband passed away. The friend had a bad knee and had given up tennis long ago. And so the contact fades. She did complain about it though, that no one from the tennis club asked after her. If the friend paid her a visit, it was for either Maria's birthday or her own, so twice a year. Then the friend would stand, cake in hand, on the doorstep, while Maria slid open four separate bolts. You heard the sofa being shoved aside. The break-in had made her mistrustful. Maria preferred to pay cash for things, so the thieves had hit the jackpot. Since then she would, after carefully bolting the door, slide the sofa against it. It was one of those sofas that could fold open. She would open it and put the vacuum cleaner on top. They needed a crane to get her out of the house, because the police couldn't get the front door open.

The friend had telephoned one Wednesday, for a birthday, but there was no answer. On Thursday she called again, and Friday too. Always at a different time of day. Still no answer. The telephone hung in the front hall. Of course, if Maria had the TV on, she wouldn't hear the phone ring. Maria liked watching television, and had just bought a new one. What a to-do *that* was, the friend says, Maria always paid cash for things – or have I told you that already? – anyway, when her old TV gave out she bought a new one, at Megapool. Two weeks later the electronics chain went bankrupt: there you are, a new TV under warranty, and you've paid cash for it. The friend became worried. On Friday afternoon she heard from the funeral insurance company that Maria had passed away. Her late husband had set up the policy for her. Take care you've got your affairs in order, he'd said. So on 1 June Maria joined a funeral collective. She stipulated that she wanted to be cremated. Her husband is buried in the Nieuwe Ooster as well, in his own grave. But she did not want to join him. Gave up her burial rites. The funeral insurance people told the friend that the cremation was on Monday. Seeing as there was no traceable next of kin, they turned over the organization of the funeral to Social Services. And now it was Monday, the friend says, in conclusion, and here she was.

We go into the chapel. The unseen organist plays for our small audience; the organ is properly warmed up today, despite, or thanks to, the bitter chill outside. Judith Herzberg recites her poem, with a brief introduction in which she thanks the friend for coming. And says that she had nothing on which to base her poem for Maria except assumptions.

* * *

We all must live
with our own dead
until we too –

And then
we end
in other's heads.

And so it goes.

But you, Maria,
Petronella van Kempen,
née de Wildt

are not in any heads
at all.
You are forever

lost. You knew
it too and welcomed
it perhaps?

Who knows?
Six weeks
before

your eighty-sixth,
you made it known:
no grave for me.

That's all
I know of you,
besides

that one green
envelope which is
my only clue.

The envelope was empty.
When
did such emptiness

set in?
You were once six!
You used to skip.

You used to kiss.
You married too.
You were a wife.

Was there discord
or even hate
or was there deep

but wasted love,
a love so great
it left a void

behind?

If you could see
us standing here,
what would you say?

Would you have thought,
'Oh, woman, mind
your own beeswax'?

As I suspect
you may have done,
I'll hold my tongue.

Judith Herzberg, translated by David Colmer

As the third piece of music is played, the friend, overcome with emotion, leaves the chapel. When the music is finished we join her in the reception room. The coffin remains behind, on its own. She asks if she can go back in, to say goodbye. That it had to come to this, she sniffs. For a moment I'm afraid she means the poem, but no, that's not it. She thought it was beautiful, really, the way it was all taken care of, it's just the confrontation with one's own imminent end that makes it so sad. In that case, then, go ahead.

Dickson Imonjie Ukhuedoba

'A flawless young face that will never again see the sun rise'
Duty poet: Alfred Schaffer

On 13 October 2005, at half past nine in the morning, the body of a Nigerian man was found in a parking space on Hofgeest, a street in the Amsterdam suburb of Bijlmer. He was in possession of a Spanish identity card; most likely he had temporary residence status there, or was at least registered as an asylum seeker. His Spanish lawyer was contacted. The Nigerian Embassy said they were too busy to trace any possible next of kin.

The man was a body-packer: in his function as drug courier, he had swallowed a number of packets or capsules of illicit drugs, and died as a result of one of the packets rupturing in his body. His name was Dickson Imonjie Ukhuedoba. He was born on 25 May 1977.

I turn into the Nieuwe Ooster at five past ten, park my bicycle and, as usual, head for the small chapel, where I am directed back to the main entrance.

Yesterday I was here as well, for an art project. The cemetery had been illuminated in fairytale splendour by a good thousand candles. Today, in the hesitant sunshine of yet another spring-like day when it should be autumn, there is no evidence of yesterday's event. Everything has been cleared out and tidied up. I greet the officiant, who I've always called Mr. Nijman: today, all of a sudden, his name turns out to be Assenbach. Nothing lasts forever. As 10:15 approaches, I prepare to ring Alfred Schaffer, but before I've found him in my address book, he hurries into sight. All present and accounted for. Now we just have to wait for the grave to be readied. The preparations have not yet been completed: apparently the art project gave rise to a minor backlog. Mr. Nijman – after all, this is what I've always called him – asks if he should close the coffin lid. Social Services said the coffin could remain open, in case some friends of our man show up, although no one does. We go inside, there he is, lying in his coffin, silent as death: a flawless young man, strong jaw line, eyes closed, full lips, broad, ample mouth. The unwrinkled, waxy texture of the dead man's skin imbues him with an otherworldly beauty. We're taken aback to see him lying there like that. Such a handsome fellow. Such a crying shame.

The chapel organist confers with us about the music. He hasn't played the 'Largo' by Handel for some time, and fancies doing so now. A quarter of an hour later than planned, he can start. Then Alfred walks to the front, places his left hand on the coffin and, his back to the audience consisting of the officiant, the four pallbearers, the organist, and myself, addresses its occupant tenderly:

WISH YOU WERE HERE

You matter again, danger lurks in the song, days shorten.
Until you disappeared. A hearty breakfast of two fried
    eggs and
bacon and toast, a slice of tomato, that view of a carpark:

you'll have to go it alone from here on we're afraid, in this
    daylight
you no longer belong to our world. In the eye of the storm
    – you've seen
the pictures, full alert before all hell breaks loose.

Now you'll make money in your sleep, now return was
   possible. Watched, whispered about,
through the mud to that little field where you scored twice
and then a party and everyone happy and everything
   allowed and no obligations,

no profundities to crack. The waitress asks if you want
   more coffee,
we approach the war zone. Your mother peering into the
   distance to see where you are,
when you get home there'll be hell to pay. You didn't escape
   anything,

there has been contact, now when you take to the street,
   this heart will petrify.
Today you were the first person to see the sun rise.

Alfred Schaffer, translated by Michele Hutchison

His voice is emotional, as though he's startled by the
intimacy of the face in the coffin. Then he returns to his
seat, the organist enters with his second piece of music,
and closes with 'Somewhere Over the Rainbow'. From
behind the lectern, Mr. Nijman expresses his dismay at the
senseless loss of this young life. Sunlight peeks through
the chink in the doors, a moth flutters restlessly around
the halogen lamps illuminating the coffin, and when the
doors open it disappears outside. We get up and follow the
coffin and the moth outdoors into the beautiful morning.
We don't have far to walk: the short-term graves are close
to the large chapel. We observe our moment of silence,
Nijman again underscores the tragedy of this end, and
Alfred adds: 'I hope someone misses him.' We walk back
for coffee; Schaffer asks for, and gets, a cup of tea. Time to
move on. As we leave the chapel, a new party is preparing

to enter: a group of thirty, forty people, at its centre a man crying uncontrollably.

'Incredibly intense,' Alfred says when we say our goodbyes a few minutes later. 'Strange just to go back to work now, as though nothing's happened.' I cycle slowly down the Middenweg, past the spot where Theo Van Gogh was murdered, almost a year ago now. A film crew putters about, the parking space where he had lain has been cleared. Two hideous yellow signs have been banged onto rough wooden sticks on cement feet and connected by red-and-white barricade ribbon. 'Keep space free from 11/1 onward', declare the black stick-on letters. The ribbon travels diagonally downward to an *amsterdammetje*, that ubiquitous knee-high parking bollard, a sloppily-tied knot ending in a ragged tail of frayed plastic. An orgy of indifferent, makeshift materials. Handiwork is handiwork. Why did the parking space have to be kept free? You don't know. You don't know if someone has thought about how this place should look, a year later. Or if it's just a completely random collection of attributes that simply gets assigned to such situations. Road works, loading zone. It is so ugly that it's almost attractive, garish in its bareness; we can't make it look any better than this. This is not an aesthetic place. If you think about it long enough, eventually you don't have to think about it anymore. Tonight, half the country will see this terrible spot once again on the evening news and current events programmes. The barricade ribbons flapping meekly in the chilly wind, those slapdash signs; tomorrow they'll probably set up a crush barrier. Then folks can decorate the spot further with bunches of flowers still in their cellophane, basically turning it into a mountain of plastic, together with teddy bears, cigarettes, cans of beer, candles, angry letters, photocopied pictures of the victim, and then lean nonchalantly over the crush barrier to admire all the junk. A few days later, once the flowers have rotted in their wrappers, everything will be cleared away. As I pass the scene of the calamity, I think that the simplest and most effective monument would be to place a parking-space-sized mirror on the asphalt, polish the mirror daily, and never again will anyone dare park on that sinister, thin sheet of sky-ice.

Back home, I make myself a cheese sandwich, and thumbing through last week's newspaper as I eat, a small item catches my eye. Hofgeest, parking space, the body of an unknown man. That spot will not be memorialized, not be roped off: nothing happened here. I see before me the flawless young face that will never see the sun rise again.

Chengian Chen

'Memory card'
Duty poet: Maria Barnas

Late last week we got word of two lonely funerals, one on Monday and one on Tuesday. The funeral on Monday 27 March 2006 is for Chengian Chen, born in Fujian, China, died in Onze Lieve Vrouwe Hospital, Amsterdam. I have the feeling the weatherman promised more sun than is actually shining this morning. The clouds look heavy enough to generate some serious precipitation. I've got my winter coat with me, but in the end it's too warm. I really should buy a raincoat, a proper, long raincoat – waterproof, but not too heavy. I cycle into the cemetery in plenty of time, and in no need of a raincoat.

Mr. Nijman, the officiant whose name is really Assenbach, is standing at the entrance gate holding a small digital camera. I greet him with a slap on the shoulder of his grey winter overcoat. He is going to take pictures of the ceremony, he says. The pictures will be sent to China along with the ashes.

Mr. Chen resided illegally in the Netherlands for quite some years. In 1993, his request for a residence permit for himself and his family was denied. His wife and children returned to China, but Chen remained behind, so officially he had no fixed address. During a fire on 14 March 2006 in the boarding house on the Valkenburgerstraat where he and several other undocumented migrants lived, he apparently jumped from a third-floor window. He died five days later as a result of his injuries. The Justice Department released his body two days after that. The fire, it seems, made the news: an item on TV, an item in the paper. The building was allegedly traced to the owner of the Sea Palace, an immense floating Chinese restaurant in an inlet of the Amsterdam harbour.

At the request of the Chinese Embassy, Chen will be cremated. In due course, the Embassy will pay for his ashes to be sent back home to his family. In Amsterdam, cremation is possible at one of two cemeteries: Westgaarde or the Nieuwe Ooster. Today it is the latter. Mr. Nijman will take pictures of the ceremony, so that Chen's wife and children can see what the chapel at the Nieuwe Ooster, where we will leave Mr. Chen behind, looks like. He has already taken a picture of the sign with the opening hours.

I park my bicycle, and notice Maria Barnas standing at the entrance to the large chapel. She walks a bit stiffly, has pulled something in her leg. A ligament or something, whatever, I'm no good at illnesses. She explains the difference between a tear and a strain. 'Uh-huh. And is it bandaged?' I ask. No, it's not bandaged. 'Must not be too bad, then,' I mumble.

She tells me she's seen a grave with a car on it. 'It's close by.' This I've got to see, a grave with a car on it. We walk slowly, she with a slight limp. It turns out to be a shiny black slab of marble under which a Roma family has created a glorious final resting place: the gravestone is etched with a recent model of a Mercedes with doors opened invitingly, man and wife posing on either side, he on the driver's side. They do not appear to be planning to get into the car. Even if you have a really expensive car you still have to fold yourself double to get in. Nor do they give the impression of just having got out. They are simply standing there next to it. The license plate, instead of a registration number, has the owner's name on it. No doubt about it: it is their car. They wouldn't be standing next to some random automobile. Maybe that's why the doors are so wide open. You don't do that with someone else's car.

We amble back to the chapel. We've been assigned the

large chapel. This means there's live organ music. The chapel can seat fifty people, or take a hundred standing. Mr. Nijman, whose real name is Assenbach, joins us. 'Let's wait for a bit,' he thinks out loud. 'The next funeral only starts at quarter past eleven.' Nobody from Social Services yet. And no friend either. Last Friday, Van Bokhoven thought maybe a friend might come. That's what the Embassy had said, that a friend might come. A friend. Later, I thought: or the owner of the floating restaurant. Or the housemates. Van Bokhoven reckoned they wouldn't dare. What if a police van were suddenly to pull up at the cemetery entrance? We wait a little longer. Then we jointly decide that no one else, including the police van, will come.

We go inside and hang up our warm coats on the coat rack. Maria does, in fact, have a raincoat, a black one. Nijman – it's just what I've got used to calling him by now – has given the organist carte blanche with the choice of music. 'The organist appreciates that,' he says, 'otherwise he'll sit there playing "Ave Maria" and "Amazing Grace" all day long.' He has already started when we enter the chapel. 'La Montanara'. I know that song. I have to dig deep to recall the lyrics: 'Up there in the mountains, amid forests and valleys of gold, amid rugged rocks there echoes a love song', and then something about 'silver streams' and 'a small, sweet abode'. Halfway through I lose track of the melody line. Maybe it's another song after all.

Then, fortunately, it's over. Nijman goes first, welcoming those present. Then he asks Ms. Barnas to come forward. She stands next to the coffin and speaks, with a more timorous voice:

Neither houses with towers of prices and slanting
banners in the window, back gardens and sun lounges
opening doors and a silver bus
driving into a future; nor the umbrella

with its heart burst open in the wastepaper basket
nor the jaded palm plant on the ground floor
can carry me. Can't someone get rid of it
faded and broken it adorns nothing and no one.

Like rain I will fall down the façade and set
a foot in the void. If they ask me who I am
I tell them the smoke drives skies into my heart.

They believe they didn't know me
but if they must, they'll calmly point out the house
where I lived: the one where no one answers the door.

Maria Barnas, translated by Donald Gardner

She lays her poem, folded into quarters, on the coffin,
sits back down. I suspect Mr. Nijman, who stood at the back
of the chapel, couldn't entirely follow it. Now the organ
plays 'Somewhere Over the Rainbow'. This one, I know.
'Somewhere over the rainbow, blue birds fly / Birds fly over
the rainbow / Why then, oh why can't I?' But here too I lose
track. ''Tis is the last rose of summer / Left blooming alone,'
my mind wants to continue, but that's not right. Then the
final number, 'Dreamland': I'll take you to my dreamland.
Now I'm sure of it.

Nijman stands, leans over and suggests in a whisper that
we walk in a circle around the coffin. We simultaneously

nod yes, take our place behind him, and follow him at a solemn pace around the coffin, stopping at the head end to bow, and then continue on to the coffee room. The poem stays behind. The officiant fights back the urge to pick up the folded sheet of paper from the coffin, as a sort of lost-and-found article. 'Is the poem supposed to be cremated along with the deceased?' he asks. Maria nods. The coffee lady, who has opened the doors to the reception room, takes a few more pictures of us as we leave the chapel in single file.

We install ourselves in the otherwise empty reception room; meanwhile, the rack with our coats has been wheeled in. Nijman has retrieved the camera from the coffee lady. We should have a look, he says. This morning, at the funeral home where Chen had been laid out, he took a picture of him, of his face. And also one of the visitation room where the body had been laid out. Two candles alongside the coffin.

Decent.

We discuss the fire, and how Mr. Chen met his end. According to Maria, he did not actually jump out of the window, but tried to climb down the drainpipe, and fell. She went to look at the building. I cycled past it this morning as well. The damage doesn't look so bad. A scorched smudge around the third-story windows. The glass isn't even cracked or shattered. The windows in the rest of this row of shabby houses, here and there with a frayed patch of cloth behind them, are sooty too, from the cars that emerge from the tunnel from Amsterdam North, under the IJ harbour, relieved to breathe fresh air.

I then cycled further, under the threatening clouds, the winter coat draped over my handlebars. Maria had asked around there this weekend. At a nearby hotel, no, they didn't know him. A massage salon, yes, there they did remember him, and later they didn't, weren't sure. The girls at the salon knew about the drainpipe.

Mr. Nijman confirms that the dead man wore a peaceful

expression. His face was unscarred, perhaps he had fallen backwards. He illustrates with a hand gesture how the neck can snap in the event of a backward fall. In that case it doesn't even need to have been from very high.

As he hands his camera to Barnas, who says she knows how to retrieve the pictures from the memory card (because Nijman himself has no idea), he explains his hesitation to say any more this time, at the coffin. 'Usually I say something like "may the angels accompany you", but you never know what the Chinese prefer.' Maria guesses: 'Happy hunting grounds?' 'No no, the happy hunting grounds, that's for American Indians,' I contradict. 'Gardens, then?' Maria suggests. 'That's it, gardens,' I say, 'they go to a big garden with those flowers, a kind of water lily – lotus flowers, a pond. That sounds right.' My proposal is met with unanimous approval. Now, at last, I understand why Chinese restaurants always have an aquarium. I ask Nijman what music the organist was playing. I thought I heard 'La Montanara', I sing a snippet of it. Nijman doesn't know. He'll ask.

By now the camera's internal memory has revealed its secrets. We see a woman standing in a kitchen. 'My wife,' says Nijman. 'I was just checking that the camera worked.' Then comes a picture of the silver hearse, half hidden behind the hedge. There is also a picture of Mr. Nijman himself looking in through a window. There is a blurry photo, betraying the photographer's shaky hand, of what looks like the chapel with the coffin. That's all. 'The rest'll be on the memory card, I guess,' Nijman reassures us. 'At least, *if* there's a memory card in it.' On the top of the camera is a sticker confirming that the camera can hold a memory card, so there must be a slot for it somewhere. But we don't dare look for the slot.

Nijman has made a list of the music; I guessed right. But halfway through, the organist segued into a different song. 'Danny Boy'. 'Somewhere Over the Rainbow' bled into 'The Last Rose of Summer', and 'Dreamland' into

'Memories'. Aha. 'So it was actually more of a potpourri,' Barnas concludes. 'A potpourri,' she repeats, savouring the word. It makes you think of air freshener, the cheapest kind of air freshener, the kind not even the manufacturer knows what it smells like. We finish our coffee, say our goodbyes. I put on my too-warm coat, and cycle slowly home. The sky is briefly threatening. Doesn't divulge a thing.

Antoon Johannes Wessel

'You held your breath whenever a car stopped at your front door'
Duty poet: Erik Lindner

Today, a Wednesday, a fine, cold, clear Wednesday, 5 April 2006, we are going to bury a man who lay dead, unnoticed, for about three weeks in his Amsterdam apartment. Anton Johannes Wessel. Born on 18 May 1928 in Amsterdam, found on the 28 March of this year. The fire department had to hoist his lifeless body through the window of his fourth-floor flat. He will be buried at St. Barbara. The garbage in his house is piled at least a metre high. This makes it impossible to enter the flat in the normal manner, namely through the front door. The flat is home to a sizeable mouse and rat population. One may presume that the body served as their victuals. The city health department, the police, the estate services (which organize personal liquidation sales), the municipal department of funerals, the owner of the apartment complex – all these agencies tried to pass the necessary clean-up to the other guy, the one citing public health, the other arguing the worthlessness of the flat's contents.

The man received a weekly telephone call from staff at the city health department, to check whether he was still alive. This is called a 'safety net', a telephone service also given to those who categorically refuse any form of hands-on assistance and / or welfare. After the third week in a row that the telephone is not answered, the police are called in to have a look.

That's how it went. The details are as gruesome as they are interchangeable. The isolation of this man, in whose house the telephone rang once a week for the past several years, was complete. Maybe he conversed with his little scurrying friends. Maybe he just preferred it this way. We know nothing of his happiness.

Marital status: single. There is no known family. Last Saturday, the city's department of funerals placed an ad in two daily newspapers. Today, Wednesday, as I arrive quite early at the cemetery, I encounter an older man in the reception room. He is wearing a dusty hat and is a friend of the deceased. They used to drink coffee together sometimes, he says, at the Looier antique market, always on Wednesdays. He liked going to the Looier. For a while Mr. Wessel collected Russian silver. He lost all of it. His over-full apartment had been cleared out once before, because it had reached breaking point. Two of those fellows with shaved heads came, sent by some council department or other, the man tells me; they said it was all going straight into the incinerator, even though they knew there was Russian silver among it. Yes, Anton did have money, sure he did, he had a decent pension, but he'd always been a thrifty man. Because of the war. At the end of the war he was arrested. When he was freed he walked with a loaf of bread under his arm to the Panama Quay, and his toes froze off. The old man with the dusty hat had been to Wessel's place before, to his half-apartment. They drank coffee there too, in the kitchen, because there was nowhere else to sit or stand. It wasn't very strong coffee.

Then Van Bokhoven arrives in his own car, a Ford Ka. A cute, pudgy little car. The company car, he says, is a Toyota Corolla. He recently read on the Internet that it was supposed to have been a Honda, but it's not; this Honda is, in fact, a Toyota. Duly noted. We go outside to smoke; we remark that it's cold out, nice and sunny but freezing cold. Van Bokhoven had to scrape the Ka's windscreen this morning. The hearse arrives, with a stretch funeral limo behind it. Mr. Nijman gets out. This was his only choice, he says, it's his lift back. Eight pallbearers stand prepared to receive the coffin, which will be carried. As it is slid out of the hearse, a penetrating odour of chemical potpourri wafts out of the vehicle with it. It assaults the mucous membranes. I sneeze. Now the thin, endlessly tall figure of the duty poet walks into the cemetery. Once we have sucked in the last of our cigarettes, Van Bokhoven concludes, that's everybody, then. The choice of music is settled: Vivaldi, absolutely, with the friend voting for 'Spring'. Autumn's nice too, I suggest, but he insists on spring. Spring is ten minutes long, you know. We'll put it at the end, he concedes at last. Then we can carry the coffin out while it's playing. We go inside. Grieg's 'Morgenstimmung', Nijman's No. 1 tune, is already playing. We seat ourselves in the tight, narrow pews. Duty poet Erik Linder to the right of the aisle; the friend with the dusty hat, Van Bokhoven, and myself to the left, the entire company in the first row.

When the morning mood has passed, Nijman comes forward and gives the floor to the poet, who squeezes his lanky body out of the pew and stands upright, directly in front of the coffin. He speaks.

A. WESSEL

Your name still stands beside the bell
on a door right opposite a new-build block
in a gentrified street you weren't evicted from.
The windows of your flat are draped with sheets,
things are stacked against some shelves.
I see tins of paint and boxes and bottles.

They've just sandblasted the façade,
new lampposts light up the street.
There's still the plumber at the corner. Two hummocks
in the pavement. A playground: climbing-frame slide
    sandpit
covered with a tarp. A bench with lines of verse.
A stone table inlaid with a draughtboard and goose-game.

I know, Meneer Wessel. This has happened.
What's the point of me saying it? Nobody
has upended your bed. The mouse-feet
grazing your trousers tickled like a girl's hand.
Here I stand talking to a box while you battled
mould, stench and fire. You didn't pull through.

You'd always be shifting your things. You'd walk as far as
    the end
of the street. Past the shop selling window-glass and paint
    supplies.
To the supermarket and back again, three flights up. You'd grab
the banister and haul yourself upwards. Put the bag
a few steps higher with your free hand. And hold
your breath if a car stopped by the front door.

Erik Lindner, translated by Francis R. Jones

58

Then we hear the 'Air' by Bach, and Nijman steps forward again, asks the friend with the hat, who earlier had indicated his desire to say a word at the grave, if he wouldn't rather do so now. At the grave, he explains, it can be rather noisy, from trains and such. Friend nods and approaches the lectern, grasps it with both hands and runs his hands cautiously over the wooden edge of the pedestal. He has left his hat on the pew. Then he speaks, about the war, the bread, the toes, and how intelligent Anton was, a master printer who was also well-versed in the Greek alphabet. About how he was later engaged on a cruise ship, where he was in charge of the printed menus and the captain's announcements. He spent years travelling. China, Japan, New York. And at the end he puttered around Amsterdam again. He sums up the genetic traits that had forced Anton into a solitary existence, and remarks that he would have preferred to be buried in Zeist, he knew of a nice cemetery there, but this was fine too, and in closing he thanks the city for the kind words and the smartly laid-on funeral. The chemical perfume slowly gives way to the unmistakable smell of decay. Then 'Spring' jangles through the chapel. Eight pallbearers slowly wheel the coffin outside, where it is shouldered. We walk to Anton's final resting place. The flowers are removed from the coffin. We observe a moment of silence. The friend has put his hat back on, and now he has both hands free, he places his flowers onto the coffin. Then it is lowered all the way to the bottom of the pit. He is here for good.

Name Unknown

'The genius detectives needed a week to reach the conclusion
that he didn't do it himself. Especially tricky,
pouring that concrete from underneath'
Duty poet: F. Starik

From Social Services I hear this: the police have been on the case for a good month now, but the investigation has been inconclusive. 'We have nothing – absolutely nothing.' Man, discovered by the police at a sub-let address at the A. W. Grootehof in Osdorp on 27 July 2006. No age, no nationality. At first I'm given the name of the detective in charge of the case, but one minute later Mr. Mahmood from Social Services calls me back to say I'm not to phone the police for more information. 'That could get me into hot water.' After all, there is no information available. And whatever information there is won't be released.

In the course of the morning I google together these details: 'The dead man found by the police on Thursday morning in a flat on the A. W. Grootehof in Amsterdam-Osdorp appears to have met a violent end. This is the conclusion of an autopsy carried out by the Netherlands Forensic Institute, the Amsterdam police reported on Friday. The identity of the man "could not yet be one hundred percent ascertained", according to a spokesperson. Police investigated after somebody attempted contact with the victim, but received no response. Upon entering the flat, officers immediately encountered a suspicious situation. The body had lain in the house for some time, but due to the ongoing investigation, police declined to specify for how long. Initially, detectives were not able to determine whether the body was that of a man or a woman. Further investigation will hopefully determine the cause of death.' An item, dated 28 July, in *De Telegraaf*.

A weblog offered this cryptic pronouncement: 'The newspaper reported that his hands and feet had been bound with zip ties, and that there was a plastic bag over his head. So the genius detectives needed a week to reach the conclusion that he didn't do it himself. Especially tricky, pouring that concrete from underneath.' I have no idea what they're talking about: pouring concrete from underneath. But it does sound tricky.

The autopsy was performed by the Netherlands Forensic Institute. They do not give out any information. Funeral Home Zuid, where the body was then brought and coffined, says that at this advanced stage of decomposition there is, in any case, little left to be seen of the body. A person, presumably.

Tuesday. The rain is so gentle it's almost imperceptible. Mr. Nijman, our officiant, is in an unusually sunny mood, in his grey suit. He thinks my suit is fine too, although he misses the tie. 'No, I'm no good at ties,' I say, 'and besides, I don't even own one.'

That's not entirely true. I ponder the only tie I possess, one I inherited from my favourite uncle. There's a Jacob's ladder printed on it, actually pretty appropriate, but it's meant ironically, a comic-strip thing, not really suitable for a funeral.

By now Nijman is admiring the gnarled corkscrew hazel, with its sadly wrinkled leaves – only last week Degenkamp had so lavishly sung its praises, marvelled at how well it had grown during this wet late-summer weather, which has more or less drowned everything on my own balcony. Nijman confesses that last winter he had planned to snip off a bunch of bare branches from the corkscrew hazel, and put them in a vase at home as decoration. It's really pretty, you know, he says. But it earned him a reprimand from Degenkamp: that's bad form.

Ali Mahmood from Social Services arrives by bicycle; the hearse pulls up and two men in jeans, who observe our small company from a distance, amble our way. 'That'll be the police,' Mahmood reckons, 'judging from their expression.' He is entirely correct. Two men in their forties, one with brushlike grey hair, the other nearly bald, both with a moustache. They introduce themselves. Daane, I recognize the name from Mahmood's initial report. 'You're investigating the case?' I enquire. There is something pained about his look. He nods. 'And still no identity.' He shakes his head. 'Age?' Now he does something in between nodding and shaking. The other detective, whose name I forget the instant it is uttered, reports that it is probably a black man, somewhere between the age of thirty and forty. Probably. Somewhere.

He speaks of a criminal background, says that no one in those circles would talk to the police, only then to fall silent himself. The grave number, though, he would like to have. Degenkamp takes out his papers. The detectives both know the dossier number by heart. A nineteen-digit number. Degenkamp writes down the grave number in the folder with that long number on it. Now the data has been linked. This man can be found. One day.

We go inside. I haven't brought any music with me. Couldn't come up with anything appropriate. Degenkamp opts for the *Peer Gynt Suite*. He has put on the music so softly that I nearly get up, three times, because I don't hear anything, and then the violins enter in the distance again. Nijman walks forward. Expresses his thanks to those present for being present, albeit in a purely professional capacity. Perhaps, he muses, this man had a wife and children. 'In that case, I hope he will be identified.' He shoots an admonishing glance at the detectives, appears to sink into thought, composes himself, and gives the floor to the poet, who recites his words slowly, emphatically, with restrained emotion. Looks, while reading, alternately at the

coffin and into the chapel, glancing up from his paper, as
though following his words with his eyes.

HUMAN

We won't impose a name on you.
Forget your sex. We'll skip those final hours.
The last face you ever saw.

We promise it was so much better once.
You walked beneath a black sky.
Someone punched your lights out.

In darkness you were found again,
picked up, prodded, weighed.
Someone held your hands.

The detective, the nimble fingers
of the forensic lab, the departmental
forms. They bag up the remains.

A label on the bag, a label
with a number, a label with no name:
you have to get that back yourself.

Someone shuts the coffin. The contents:
presumably human. The black lamp
to light your path was dimmed.

Let us say goodbye, nameless one.
Not Mohammed, not Dieudonné, not John,
but have a safe journey and walk in the sun.

F. Starik, translated by David Colmer

I bow to the deceased. Return to my seat. Tuck the poem back into the pocket of my jacket. Something by Saint-Saëns timidly emerges from the sound system. Behind us we hear the door to the chapel open. It is Tuesday. On the first Tuesday of the month, St. Barbara offers an open memorial service at ten o'clock, when anyone can come to grieve for a lost loved one. I hear the loud crinkle of a plastic bag.

I look over my shoulder. An elderly woman has taken a seat on a pew about halfway back. She goes on crinkling vigorously. I don't look again. Then I hear footsteps heading towards the front of the chapel, and a moment later she glides back into my field of vision, audibly deposits a coin into the metal box, takes a candle and lights it.

She takes no notice of the others present, nor does she pay any heed to the coffin. She has clearly come for herself, not for us. Not for the deceased. She returns to her seat, and resumes her labours with the plastic bag.

The detective with the pained expression now looks overtly behind him, allowing his sorrowful gaze to rest squarely on the woman. She is not bothered, disregards him entirely. Mind your own business. During the third musical selection, from the genre 'light classical', the pallbearers come forward. We stand, watch as the pallbearers roll the coffin outside, then follow them, past the woman, who remains calmly seated, the plastic bag on her lap.

We do not speak on the way. Once at the grave we observe our moment of silence, the coffin is lowered, and that's that. My son is at home, it's his first day of school. Junior high school. He will pick up his books. He will be given a timetable. They will show him how to cover your books. He will cover them. He is looking forward to it. A whole new world is opening up for him.

64

Name Unknown

'It's more the idea of coffee'
St. Barbara Cemetery, Friday 20 April 2007, 10 a.m.
Duty poet: Neeltje Maria Min

There are two lonely funerals this morning: at nine o'clock we laid to rest Mario Agus, an elderly Italian man, found dead in his apartment, nothing out of the ordinary. First duty poet is Catherina Blaauwendraad, and she executes her task admirably, as always.

The news item had already appeared in my inbox last week. Apparently someone foresaw that this would end as a lonely funeral: 'BODY OF BABY FOUND IN AMSTERDAM CANAL. A local resident found the body of a baby in the water of the North Holland Canal, on the Buiksloterdijk in Amsterdam.' That was Wednesday 11 April, but the police only made it known two days later. Police confirmed that it was a full-term baby that 'must have been in the water for some time. The passerby noticed a plastic bag amongst the washed-up litter, and pulled it ashore with a rake, whereupon the bag tore open and he discovered the body.'

Ali Mahmood from Social Services adds the following information: the baby was most likely born at 39 weeks, therefore full-term. Found on 11 April at 4:30 p.m., across from Buiksloterdijk 198. Brought to the VU hospital; the body was released on Monday and transferred to Funeral Home Zuid.

From there, the infant makes its last journey to St. Barbara. The police will not say whether it was a boy or a girl. Nor do they want to say how long the child had been in the water. A comprehensive forensic investigation is underway, and an autopsy has been performed. Additionally, police have made inquiries in the neighbourhood. They still have no leads as to the infant's identity. 'We're reluctant to divulge information that could hamper the investigation. We waited before issuing yesterday's report in order to secure our line of inquiry.' Investigators are searching for the baby's mother and for witnesses or persons who can offer any information as to the identity of the young victim. On an online news site I find a video item by the local television station AT5, in which neighbourhood resident Roef Bakker tells how he happened upon the baby. He regularly tidies up the canal's edge, dredging up litter with his rake. 'Looks like refuse from a butcher,' he thought at first, 'but no, it's got a totally different face. And then I called the police.'

Poet Neel would like to know if it's a boy or a girl. 'That's half the battle.' Mahmood does not know. So I call the police. They hum and haw. '...In light of the ongoing inquiry...' I don't see the problem: had the mother wanted to know the sex of her child, she could have seen it. They ask for the name of the poet. They promise to get back to me.

An hour later, they do indeed ring back. The spokesperson can tell me it is a baby boy, and that he had been in the water for between ten and twenty days. Nationality or race, he can't or won't say. Was the child stillborn, or killed with intent, like people disposed of a litter of unwanted kittens in the old days? That all falls under 'offender's knowledge'. Incidents of this type often elicit false confessions. So the less the public knows, the more the confessor has to guess, and they nearly always guess wrong.

On Wednesday, Mahmood phones again: the police have announced the time and whereabouts of the funeral on the television programme *Crimewatch*, which has encouraged people to attend the funeral and pay their last respects to the infant. The announcement is repeated on the local stations AT5 and RTV North Holland, in the hope that mum watches television, sees her own life, her fifteen minutes of fame. After which she throws away the baby in a plastic bag. Or does a boyfriend, a jealous ex, a housemate dispose of the dead baby? You anxiously scour the news reports, to see if it's been found yet. Then you see on TV that it *has* been found. And you hear on the news where and when you're expected at the funeral. This is why they specify the time and place in the media. It ratchets up the pressure. They can't, after all, send the mother a personal invitation. If it's well-attended, so goes the rationale, then the mother might dare to show up incognito. She can mingle inconspicuously among the flower-and-teddy bear crowd, among the cameras in search of a juicy human interest item. The emotions of the common man. There is another tactic behind all this I'm only allowed to reveal later: if the mother knows exactly where the child is buried – because it's been shown on TV – then she might come back, on her own, for a look. She won't notice the closed-circuit camera that has been mounted behind the dormer window of the chapel. And in this way she's found after all, if they're lucky. Well, lucky, that's not the word.

I decide to ask Degenkamp if we can keep the TV cameras out of the chapel. The cemetery is a public access area, there's nothing to be done about that. But an exception can be made for the funeral itself, which will be held inside. There has to be calm, a haven, a moment of quiet respect for the baby itself. Degenkamp brings it up with the police, and his department head, Kerstens, accepts the proposal 'wholeheartedly'. Neel and I discuss the music.

The tension grows. On Thursday, Van Bokhoven calls to say the preceding funeral will be pushed forward fifteen minutes. Funeral Home Zuid's decision. 'Keeping in mind the anticipated media presence,' is how Van Bokhoven formulates it. The next morning Fritz will lecture us that this is totally unacceptable. For now I see it as a clever manoeuvre to get us to relax. Gives us plenty of extra time. By nine thirty, Mario Agus will be six feet under.

There's time for a smoke outside, in the sun. I've still got some cigarettes left over from my talk yesterday. I make use of them. When I give a talk, I buy myself cigarettes rather than rolling tobacco. Because so often you have to smoke hurriedly and in awkward spaces. No time to fuss with roll-ups which take up precious time. 'So they call this healthy?' the big, good-natured pallbearer Jan wonders, 'making people smoke outside now?' I ask him if he's also to be a pallbearer at the forthcoming funeral. I realize too late that there's nothing to bear. The officiant will carry that little shoebox of a coffin himself. Last week, Jan tells me, they had a coffin holding a 200-kilo man. They needed a forklift to hoist him into the grave. Now that's heavy. His hands outline a coffin the size of a bungalow.

First the police detectives arrive, about six of them, both sexes, each carrying a teddy bear. They've got a closet full of teddy bears there, Fritz says. 'Vice squad. You can tell at a glance.' A while later a mobility scooter carrying an old lady glides up noiselessly. She parks, gets off. She seems to be able to walk with no problem. She is here for the funeral. Is this the place. God Almighty. She looks as if she has spent the whole night weeping. Another teddy bear. Then Kerstens and Van Bokhoven arrive in the company car. Kerstens remarkably well dressed, pinstripe suit, black with white pinstripes. Van Bokhoven in the customary Van Bokhoven blue. Neeltje walks up in her formless frock. Clothes, she once told me, are best bought used: then you know how they'll hold up in the wash and they've lost some of their garish colour. Catherina, who had just left the previous funeral, returns with Neeltje, out of courtesy, out of modesty. 'Here I am again.'

And there's the TV crew too. Camerawoman, sound man, a young fellow who is allowed to carry the camera stand, someone else who doesn't have to do anything at all, he's the producer. Sorry, no filming in the chapel, Kerstens explains to the head man. That's a real pity, the man says, because he was planning to make a respectful item. Would the poet care to be interviewed. 'No,' Neeltje says firmly. Would she re-read the poem outside in the cemetery, for the camera? 'I think not,' she says, just as categorically. How about a radio recording, then? Well… We look at one another. He produces a small apparatus that can be placed unobtrusively on the lectern while the poet speaks. We agree: put the apparatus in place before the service begins. The man who has nothing to do anyway is allowed inside, to keep an eye on the apparatus. In case something goes awry, suddenly. The camera stays outside.

The crowd has grown to some twenty people. A mother with a child of about five. A few elderly folks. No sign of neighbour Roef Bakker. Neeltje tells us what 'roef' means. It's that section of the coffin lid that gradually rises from the foot end to the head. She came across another unusual word while looking for the right opening for her poem: a 'donkey's burial', one attended by almost no one. My dictionary defines it as a burial in unhallowed ground.

We go into the chapel. Brahms does his work, effectively. 'Guten Abend, gute Nacht.' I sit directly behind Ger Fritz. I study his square buzz-cut, the unruly grey spikes. Neeltje walks forward. I see the apparatus lying on the lectern. She folds open her poem.

FOR YOU

Always in water
always floating
living only a moment

Who looked into your eyes
read your features
begged forgiveness

Who went outside
to push off
the plastic-bag boat

Who said one, two,
in the name of God! three

You existed, you lived
you weren't to blame

Nameless, innocent
dead in the canal
no-days-old

Rest in God's name in peace
rest rest rest in peace
in the name of your father
and your poor mother:

in peace.

Neeltje Maria Min, translated by David Colmer

Clear, calm and simple, her voice. Then Louis Armstrong begins to sing. 'When You Wish Upon a Star'. Someone sniffles. As one expects. Paul McCartney, too, gives his best. Then the officiant steps forward, takes the little coffin carefully in his arms, a white shroud over it. Everyone stands. Young Degenkamp leads, opens the doors of the chapel. We follow, into the bright sunlight.

The camerawoman shuffles backwards ahead of us. That is a skill you have to have as camera operator: to walk backwards quickly, without looking, and without jiggling the camera. It's not far to Angel's Corner, where dead children are buried. Young Degenkamp takes the coffin from the officiant, lowers it cautiously on a rope. A shovelful of sand can be tossed, and those present grasp the opportunity. Just the moment to place your teddy bear. The lady with the mobility scooter goes first. The camerawoman squats on her knees in front of the grave, recording the small crowd with that cold eye. She films from the left, from the right, from the back and from the front. Catherina and I wait hidden behind the hedge until it's over. I see the tears glisten on her cheeks. Neeltje is nowhere to be seen. When everyone is finished with the sand, when the camerawoman has immortalized the collection of teddy bears, and they proceed to interview the lady with the scooter, we emerge from our hiding place. Fritz joins us, and there's Neeltje again.

We meander through the cemetery. Fritz points out graves, tells stories. At an overturned flowerpot, Neeltje observes: 'The dead were restless last night.' They were indeed. And tonight they will be again. Catherina Blaawendraad will e-mail me later: 'I'd planned to leave. I dreaded the impending media circus. At the exit I bumped into Neeltje Maria Min, who said she'd like it if I stayed. I'm glad I did that: stay. Did you know, by the way, that Pope Benedict XVI abolished limbo for unbaptized children last Saturday? "The exclusion of innocent babies from Heaven does not seem to reflect Christ's special love for the little ones," the Pope's statement read. The centuries-old theory of limbo states that infants who die at birth or shortly thereafter do not go directly to heaven, because they have not become freed from original sin through baptism. Nor, however, do they go directly to hell, for they have committed no evil. These children will therefore enjoy eternal bliss in limbo. According to the Italian media, the Pope also took into account the high rate of abortion worldwide. Moreover, fewer and fewer children are baptized.

'But this is by the by,' Catherina continues. 'I will carry on asking myself: am I doing this for the deceased, or because of the idea that my farewell makes a difference? Not that it's a bad thing, a person needs to feel important once in a while. But still, the finest moments are the moments when you stand there and don't have to wonder if it matters. That you just feel that it matters when someone takes the trouble to stop and think of someone else. Neeltje's gentle nod at the coffin. That feeling.'

We chat a bit in the coffee room. The coffee is served by a new fellow from the caterer's, today he's smartly dressed in a blue suit with modest pinstripes, even a necktie. Min is complimented on her poem. Fine words, says the officiant. Neeltje gives everyone a personally hammered-out typescript of the poem. Dated and signed. 'The coffee's got more expensive here,' Van Bokhoven chuckles, 'forty-five euros just for that guy to show up.' 'Let's have a second cup then,' Min suggests, 'so we'll get our money's worth.' She thinks the coffee here is delicious. 'At least, not as strong as in a restaurant.' She's right. The stuff is indeed scalding hot; it's not got much taste. It's more the idea of coffee.

Back at home, I reply to Catherina: Recently I had to talk about 'the final journey' – that was what they called the programme in The Hague. Alfred Schaffer was the moderator, Anneke Brassinga and Neeltje Maria Min related their experiences as a 'duty poet'. Both see their task as a Mission, a mission one cannot refuse. You put everything aside for it. Brassinga expressed her surprise that the poets in the pool are 'assigned' four funerals; when she agreed to participate, she regarded it as a commitment for life. Only then did I realize that this is how I see it too, or rather, have come to see it. At first I thought: twenty funerals, then I'll stop. Somewhere around thirty, we set up the foundation, and it had to get up and running; okay, fifty, then. In the end it becomes part of your life, it permeates your entire consciousness. An eternal presence. Brassinga also remarked that she regards a poem for a lonely funeral purely as an incidental work, and would never include it in a collection, nor publish it elsewhere, to which she added she would be loath to revise it after the fact. Not even if she spots things in the text later on that she'd preferred to have expressed differently. The poem exists purely in the moment, she feels. I believe I think otherwise. But I'm not even sure if believing is thinking, or the other way around, whether thinking is believing. During dinner Neeltje Maria Min observed, as she stared at the table decoration consisting of a rose and a small branch in a square glass container of water, that not everything that is beautiful necessarily has to taste nice. Brassinga picks up the decoration and cautiously sniffs it. Min is right, she says. I eat a rose petal. 'Just as not everything that's tasty is necessarily beautiful,' Neeltje ratchets it up a notch, as she pokes at the greyish goop that was touted as Moroccan mezze. Later, Catherina adds, by e-mail: 'Entirely beside the point, but anyway: Ger Fritz gave me a lift home – a trip down memory lane, I expect. He grew up in the neighbourhood and went to school here. His aunts lived nearby, and his first girlfriend lived across from the old trade school. About ten years back he had to clean out my neighbour's house, he still knew which one it was. And he pointed out the shop where, as a kid, he once tried to climb between the front wall and a pillar, and got stuck. I'll never be able to walk past that shop without picturing it. Got to stop now. I've dribbled muesli on the keyboard.'

José Da Silva Almeira

'The despondency that spring just won't come.
The despondency of a self-chosen end'
Duty poet: Menno Wigman

Jose Da Silva Almeira was born on 19 October 1948 in Rio Tinta, Portugal. He lived in Middlesex, England. He had a British passport. He was married and leaves behind a 16-year-old son. He was in Amsterdam temporarily. He was found on 24 March 2008 on the De Ruyterkade, across from the Western Viaduct near Central Station, at 7:30 p.m. He will be cremated at the Nieuwe Ooster cemetery on Thursday 3 April at 3 p.m.

The body was impounded after being discovered, and then released on Friday 28 March. The man's wife came to Amsterdam for identification purposes, 'to ascertain that the deceased is her husband,' according to the bureaucratic report. 'There is no money and no insurance; transportation to England not possible. Wife requests that the police arrange cremation in Amsterdam. The ashes will be repatriated at a later date. The wife returned home on Saturday. She will not attend the cremation. The death was a suicide.'

Menno Wigman gets to work. Van Bokhoven gives him the number of the detective handling the case, who is remarkably forthcoming. Naturally he's not at liberty to divulge anything, but he does say that Mr. Almeida hanged himself in the open air, at a construction site alongside the Western Viaduct where they're building a cross-harbour tunnel. The police presume he was here looking for odd jobs. His family saw him off when he left for Amsterdam.

In the days preceding the funeral we discuss the music. 'Northern Sky' by Nick Drake, Menno suggests, that'll do it every time. I'll bring an Arvo Pärt CD with me. I consider Pink Floyd, a bit from *The Wall*, a film-music-like clip lasting barely two minutes, which starts with the words: 'Is there anybody out there?' But that's laying it on so thick. Too thick. Perhaps 'Fake Empire' by The National, but then that's maybe a bit too much pop music.

Thursday afternoon. Spring just won't come; grey, chilly day. Menno is already at the Nieuwe Ooster when I arrive. Then the officiant arrives, Mr. Veldhoen: tall, slightly stooped, grey moustache. He greets me with: 'Long time no see.' There's Van Bokhoven. He's got a whole list of communiqués. Mr. Kerstens, the head of the department, is on sick leave; it could last for a while, so an interim head has been appointed. I jot down his name on a slip of paper. Bert Kiewik. Van Bokhoven, animated, says: 'I was in your neighbourhood yesterday, across the street, number 97. A man with mobility scooter, passed away in the hospital. I looked up to see if you happened to be home. But you weren't. They've managed to track down some of the guy's family, so we don't have to do him.'

'That's a relief.' I often lock up my bike in front of said ground-floor house; the television is always on. Now the television is off. The Evangelical Broadcasting station had an item a few days ago on *Network* about folks who die alone and are only discovered much later: a man in IJmuiden who lay in his terrace house for five months. The reporter talked to the neighbours. Didn't notice anything. Another man in a railway-keeper's house in Baarn. Lay there dead for a month. Passers-by were used to giving him a wide berth: he was always just a tad too eager to strike up a conversation while the crossing was closed and you had to wait for the barriers to go up again. The man in IJmuiden had been married. His ex-wife lives in Santpoort; Menno recalls the flower lady just down the street from where he grew up. Nothing's changed, she hasn't aged a day. Perhaps there's something purifying about being around flowers all day. A while ago I got a call from one of the *Network* producers. Wanted to know if we also write Christian poetry. 'Only for girls named Maria,' I should have answered.

We go over the choice of music again. We decide to start with the 'Air', followed by Nick Drake's 'Northern Sky', and to close with 'Spiegel im Spiegel' by Arvo Pärt. 'It's a bit of a long sit,' I warn them, 'a good ten minutes.' 'We can always get up after a few minutes,' the officiant reassures us. We enter the small chapel. Bach does his work. Menno walks to the front, clears his throat into the microphone, summarizes what he knows about the deceased, reads his poem slowly, lucidly, distinctly.

THERE'S TIMES YOU ALMOST FEEL ALIVE

There's times you almost feel alive.
You book a flight, go into a city, take a room,
delude yourself you're mighty as your suitcase clicks.

A cipher comes to wipe your table clean.
A cipher straightens out your sheets, weighs up
your passport, airs your head. You are alive.

Six thousand scrambled eggs. For you. For you
the city shores up its façades and builds
new tunnels, restaurants, a new high-rise.

That evening late, you walked along the waterside.
You saw a building site and didn't get it.
What kept those stupid cranes upright?

Smaller and smaller, your foot sought out a route.
Crowds and crime! Kick back. Your tongue is loose
and makes its final point inside a well-made noose.

Menno Wigman, translated by David Colmer

'Dear Mr. Almeira,' he closes, 'sleep tight, and soundly.' Nick Drake sings his guarded song, Arvo Pärt fills the space with beads of minimalist piano notes, framed by a searching violin. We sit very still, three men in a row, legs crossed. Behind us, the officiant mans the buttons. Time seems to have been suspended. Even once the music has died out, nothing happens. Eventually the officiant walks to the front, gestures at the coffin, opens the door. Van Bokhoven stands, bows at the coffin, we all stand up, bow, retire to the coffee room. Shaking off the silence and the absence of time takes a while. We remain standing. Only when the coffee arrives do we sit. Curious, the way we sat so silently for Mr. Almeida, a good quarter of an hour, motionless.

That evening one of the large goldfish that swim around in my aquarium died. When I get home he is lying despondently on the bottom of the tank, gasping for air, it seems, his mouth moving slowly up and down, as though he's short of breath. Despondent: Menno used the word frequently that afternoon. The despondency that spring just won't come. The despondency of a self-chosen end.

Idrissa Soumalia

'Out of nowhere, and going there too'
Duty poet: Neeltje Maria Min

Idrissa Soumalia's date of birth is registered as 1 January 1962. He hailed from Ayorou, a town in western Niger. He died in the Amsterdam Medical Centre on 28 September 2008 at 2:40 p.m. when a number of drug packets he had been carrying in his body – 31 in total – ruptured. He had been taken ill in a hotel in Amsterdam-Zuidoost. He was brought by ambulance to the AMC. Medical intervention was in vain. The body was impounded, and then released some days later. It will remain in the VU hospital morgue, cooling cell 25, until the day of the funeral. He will be brought to his final resting place on Wednesday 15 October at a quarter past two, at Westgaarde Memorial Park.

Van Bokhoven from Social Services picked up the man's suitcase and personal belongings from the police station, including his mobile phone. An acquaintance of the deceased had been contacted with the request that he relay the news of Idrissa's passing to his family. The consul in The Hague, Mr. Poesiat, had spoken to this acquaintance on the phone. 'His cell phone rang repeatedly,' the consul said. 'I got someone on the line who unfortunately did not speak English. After a few minutes the phone rang again; the caller did speak English and identified himself as the brother. I told him that his brother had died. I gave him my name and telephone number, and was about to ask for his number when the connection was broken.'

The next day Van Bokhoven writes in his official report: 'I spoke with Mr. Poesiat again; yesterday he had contact with the family in Niger. The connection kept breaking. After that he called six more times, and each time he got someone different on the line. No one wants to make a decision: bury him in Amsterdam, yes or no? The consul requests postponement for one more day. He has sent a fax to the Embassy in Brussels, and they in turn have faxed the Foreign Office with the request to inform the family.'

And a few days later: 'I have again spoken to the consul, and he now says that, as there has been no reply from the family, please proceed to bury in Amsterdam, in a Muslim grave. Transporting the body to Niger would cost approximately 7000 euros. Today we received a fax from the consul with the correspondence between the consul and the Embassy. A statement has been drawn up.'

The consul thanks Van Bokhoven for his 'utmost propriety in handling the case'. And the consul expresses his sympathy to the family: 'Should anyone wish to attend the funeral, we will assist the family as best we can.'

'Justice Dept. notifies us that there is no indication Mr. Soumalia had planned to transport the drug packets to Niger.' Six pages of information roll grudgingly out of the fax machine. It's almost touching to hear the machine puffing and panting: an industrial moment. I send the papers by post to duty poet Neeltje Maria Min, who likewise gives computers a wide berth.

The poem she comes to read on Wednesday was produced on a typewriter with an overused ribbon: here and there she penned in certain letters before taking her typescript to a copy centre, on the way to Westgaarde, where I arrive on my bicycle at the precise moment she alights from the bus that has brought her this far.

We walk together into the cemetery. I tell her Van Bokhoven had called me to say that the consul will attend the funeral, and perhaps the ambassador as well; he will have to come all the way from Brussels. This appears to be the case. Van Bokhoven and Kiewik from Social Services are waiting for us at the entrance to the chapel. As we are led to the waiting room, we pass a group of Surinamers gathering for a funeral; there is a brass band, the bell of the sousaphone covered with a black cloth. I am curious as to whether we shall soon hear the trumpets sound.

The waiting room, where the consul, a heavy-set man, and the ambassador and his assistant, both clearly from Niger, are waiting for us. The officiant enters first. An officiant I've not met before, with transparent-framed glasses, a strange woollen black coat above smooth black trousers. His shoes, also black, have a playful, and only upon closer inspection, wavy bordeaux-red pattern: a man who has mastered the concept of a 'dignified tread'.

Niceties and praise are exchanged. When we arrive, the ambassador is on the telephone with an imam, who instructs him in the requisite prayers. The officiant knows it is customary at a Muslim funeral to wheel the coffin directly to the grave, to recite the prayers there, and to cover the coffin with sand. Flowers: not necessary. Van Bokhoven accordingly decides to skip the flower arrangement, but to play the three chosen musical excerpts, and offer the opportunity for prayers at the grave. Then the ambassador hangs up, we shake hands with him and his assistant, who until now has only observed the proceedings from some distance. Kiewik explains, in English, that this is a 'special service', that a poet comes to read a poem at the funeral. The ambassador understands. He must now ritually wash his hands, then the funeral can begin.

An indifferent snippet of melancholy classical music plays as we enter. Kiewik and Van Bokhoven sit to the right of the aisle, the three emissaries to the left. I decide to sit one row back, also on the left side, and Neeltje takes a seat next to me. The ambassador spreads his hands in a gesture of blessing, begins mumbling a prayer. I motion to the back to turn off the music; it is turned down, and the ambassador's voice gets louder.

Then he is quiet for a little while. The music resumes, softly at first, then a bit louder. The ambassador mumbles another prayer. Music gets turned down again. Music, thankfully, finishes. Neeltje walks forward. She has kept her raincoat on. Buttoned all the way up.

FOR IDRISSA SOUMALIA

I wanted to be angry with you.
Not furious or resentful,
no, the usual wrath
of a mother for a son:
a loving rage, no blows.

For a long time I felt a vicarious
fear and anger. At your swallowing
what they told you. Because
you were so full of little plans.

How those plans burst.
I won't ask how you bore
those final hours, or if
you got what you deserved.

For seven last times
your motherless mobile
called to the moon:
beep – beep – beep.
Out of nowhere,
and going there too.

Neeltje Maria Min, translated by David Colmer

Now comes the second piece of music. The consul leans over to the ambassador and gives him a whispered translation of the poem, or as much of it as he could remember. We sit out the last piece of music in silence. Off we go, to the section of the cemetery reserved for Muslims There's a sign: MUSLIM. A streak of red paint has been smeared over it; its removal has not been entirely successful. At the grave, where there is a photograph of someone who recently vanished somewhat deeper into the same pit, some more prayers are recited, then the coffin is lowered. Four large shovels have been stuck into the sand heap next to it. Time to get to work. Consul, ambassador and assistant shovel the coffin out of sight. In the distance we hear brass music: unseen, the cortège of Surinamers files past, toward another grave.

Name Unknown

'A murky ditch, an ambulance, that red-and-white
barrier tape, men in reflective vests'
Duty poet: Erik Menkveld

'Report received from Officer Steers, police dept. Meer & Vaart bureau, 3 November 2008 at 12:35 p.m. Unidentified body removed from water, on the Lutkemeerweg across from house number 274. Identity still not ascertained, body released on 4 November. Buried at St. Barbara, Monday 10 November, one spade deep, section B, grave number 51.' So reads the official statement Van Bokhoven faxes me.

'SUITCASE FOUND WITH BODY INSIDE,' says *De Telegraaf* online. 'A suitcase containing the corpse of a man was found in a runnel, an irrigation ditch, parallel to the Lutkemeerweg in Amsterdam-Osdorp on Thursday afternoon. Authorities assume the deceased was the victim of a crime. Sanitation Department workers noticed the suitcase in the ditch and dragged it onto the bank, whereupon they made their gruesome discovery. Nothing is yet known of the victim's identity. The precise cause of death is presently being investigated.' The article also says that police are unwilling to report on the state of the body. An online news website also places a brief item. All items date from 10 October. Since then, no information regarding the dead man has come to light.

Thumbnail photos accompanying the items show a murky ditch, an ambulance, that red-and-white barrier tape, men in reflective vests. There is no doubt that the photo was taken in autumn. On the Monday that the unidentified man is to be laid to rest, the weather is blustery: a hard wind accompanied by heavy rain showers. I've got another appointment earlier that morning, and on the way back I am drenched within minutes. The raincoat I've hung up to dry is so waterlogged that the coat hanger breaks. I take my new funeral suit from the closet, and the hanger it came on also spontaneously snaps. When I leave the house shortly after that, the door resisting slightly because the coat rack is too full, yet another hanger breaks: today is apparently coat-hanger-breaking-day. I cycle off, despondently, but it remains dry, I do not get drenched and my bike does not fall apart.

Arriving at the cemetery, I see duty poet Erik Menkveld drive up in what my world is called a Citroën Berlingo. Other car manufacturers offer a practically identical model under a different name; it's somewhere in between a passenger car and a van, a poor man's multipurpose vehicle. The pallbearers, four of them, are standing at the gate, with a female officiant I've not seen before. New. I slalom neatly past them on my bicycle, and notice Menkveld's dark-blue car pull gingerly into the parking lot. A fantastic entrance, as though he's delivering the body himself.

A bit later, Kiewik and Van Bokhoven from Social Services arrive, as well as an anthropology student specialising in 'death and loss' who had approached the Services with the request to attend a lonely funeral. Mr. Degenkamp has new glasses, the modern kind with a sturdy frame, they look good on him. We discuss Menkveld's choice of music. The officiant is disappointed that the CDs she has brought with her will not be used. Menkveld had e-mailed me earlier in the day about his repertoire: 'I've narrowed it down to three pieces; I'm new at this so not entirely sure how they'll fit into the funeral. A five-part motet from the fifteenth century, composer unknown; for when we walk in? It lasts six minutes but can be faded out at any time. "Pranam II" by Giacino Scelsi: this one I'd like to be played in its entirety, it also lasts six minutes, so probably not suitable as entry music. And lastly, the first solo from "Compassion" by Coltrane. Goes nicely with my poem.'

A quarter past three. We have agreed that we'll enter and take our seats to the strains of the anonymous motet, which will be allowed to play out, that Erik will then read his poem, after which we shall listen to the Scelsi piece, and then will exit the chapel to the sound of Coltrane. The poet is wearing a completely black suit. He is doing this for the first time. In my briefing I informed him that the poet should be 'dressed appropriately'. That he is, although the beige suede shoes do not really go with the rest of the outfit. What if the poet only has a few pairs of shoes? He purchases a new pair when the current ones are worn out, and then wears those until they in turn are worn out. When people say: new glasses? Different haircut? he will answer: no, new shoes. They will admire his shoes. People call this 'poetic license'. When the classical voices have finished, Menkveld walks to the front and reads out his poem, almost like an accusation. Even though he possesses a pleasant voice, his words hit hard. Nothing here is between parentheses.

DISCONSOLATE HOMAGE

Did a debt get out of hand? Did you shoot off your mouth?
Or were you just an arsehole whose luck ran out? Wrong
     time,
wrong place. In a suitcase and gone. You must have been
a mighty pain in someone's neck and God knows whose,
for them to cut you off so totally from everything you were.

On the ninth of last October (I read on the Internet)
employees of the Osdorp sanitation department fished
a suitcase from a ditch and you were in it. Three weeks later
and you are nameless still. And gosh: authorities fear
the deceased may have been the victim of a crime.

I stare a while through my densely populated window
at the deserted plain of your life, picturing your childhood,
your house, your food, your music and your loves, the final
acts of violence dying on your retina, trying
to reconstruct what I was doing

in that searing moment (talking with my young
son's teacher about his progress in arithmetic).
Poetically drifting off again into simultaneity
and how little people suspect of the ruthlessness
through which they move.

Who'd do something like that? I think naively. Whoever
hacked you up and dumped you in the water like garbage
was born of woman too, they went to school,
chewed blades of grass beneath the stars and once lay
trembling beside a love they couldn't understand.

Everything you ever cherished, hoped, believed,
everything you ever suffered or experienced,
extinguished forever in that icy ditch.
It didn't get you into any print editions.
That's why I'm scraping these

words together now – not as consolation,
that doesn't help you when you're dead, but as a disconsolate
homage to the unknown life that raged through you
before it was cleared out of the way for good,
'one spade deep', in Section B, Plot 51.

Erik Menkveld, translated by David Colmer

Whereas the first piece of music felt trusted, classical, the
second turned out to be a dark, well-nigh atonal composition
from the genre 'contemporary classical', whose aim seems to
be to express profound pain, while Coltrane's 'Compassion'
bids a wildly percussive and joyous farewell to our unknown
man. Walking past the bier as we exit the chapel, I notice the
officiant's CDs: *100 Best-loved Dutch Songs*, with a photo of
crooner Jan Smit on the cover, and *The Most Beautiful Classical
Melodies*. The rain is still holding off, although I see an almost
black sky approaching from the west. We wait around the
corner as the coffin is put into place. The officiant has set us
further away than usual; next to us a small family gathering
tends a tidy grave, placing flowers and incense, real incense
like the kind you smell in church, a waft reaches us, and
then we can come closer.

Menkveld's poem is anchored to the lid with three little
heaps of sand. Then the coffin is lowered. Each of us throws
on a shovelful of sand. We walk back to the chapel. I'm
curious how the music went over. 'It certainly was a change
of pace,' Kiewik hazards. 'But that's good too, sometimes,'
Van Bokhoven adds. Menkveld takes this opportunity to

explain his musical choice, from the anonymous madrigals, via the composer Scelsi (about whom not much is known except that his music went undiscovered for much of his career and was found in a library), to the compassion of Coltrane.

Over coffee we chat our way back to the real world, picking up some more details of a lonely funeral we conducted this past summer. A couple of unidentified divers who had turned up in the Amsterdam container port. One of the two divers, the one who was buried without his wetsuit, has now been identified. It'll appear in the papers soon, but first the detectives want to talk to his wife: seems he was married. The department that deals with personal property wants to auction off his brand-new diving equipment. Fat chance, Van Bokhoven says. It's a small world, the divers. Nobody's going to want that stuff. Not even for free.

Mr. W. G.

Born 22 November 1933, died 23 April 2013
St. Barbara Cemetery, Thursday 2 May, 11:30 a.m.
Duty poet and report: Eva Gerlach

A remarkable funeral. Afterwards, once I've returned home and want to get cracking on the report, I don't know where to start. A few hours later I e-mail Eva Gerlach. 'You know what? Maybe I won't write anything at all this time. I can't find the right tone, I don't know what to say and what not to. I'll just upload your poem, and that's that.' She writes back that she suspects W.'s son, C., who was present at the funeral, would probably like the story to be told after all. And that she is prepared to try to tell it. The son had given me his mobile phone number, which I pass on to Eva. She will keep contact these next few days with the son who, in the end, did attend his father's funeral. And yes, he would like a report to be written, and put online. What follows is Eva Gerlach's report, authorized and supplemented by C. G. himself.

[Eva Gerlach writes] Starik e-mails: 'At first, Van Bokhoven found two children in W.'s files; the local census bureau turned up six more. Of the eight, three were already deceased. All five surviving children were contacted by post; a few responded. Their stories were not good. Domestic violence, termination of parental responsibility, foster care – unwelcome memories.

'W. was married three times, and divorced three times. At the end he resided in a senior-living complex in Amsterdam North (Van Bokhoven described the apartment as "chaotic") and died in the cardiology unit of the Boven IJ hospital.'

89

When I try, in preparing for the poem, to imagine what life must have been like for W., I realize I cannot. W.'s life story has – right down to the first initial – so much in common with that of my own strange father that every time I hazard an attempt, I immediately put myself in the shoes of W.'s eight children. But it's not for them that I'm writing.

Eventually, late Wednesday night, thirty-two lines pretty much write themselves. On Thursday morning I take these lines to St. Barbara Cemetery, where I arrive – by way of exception – twenty minutes early. It is chilly, there's a brisk wind. Starik is not there yet; a man in jeans and a black sweater, motorcycle helmet in hand, leans against the door to the coffee room; some dignitaries in black are waiting to receive the hearse, which has just pulled up. When it stops, they make a deep bow: respect is the key to the ritual of the final journey.

As the coffin rolls out, the man in the jeans and black sweater approaches me. 'Are you here for him?' he asks. 'Yes,' I say. 'You too?' 'Yes,' he says, 'who are you?' At that moment I realize he is one of the children, and fervently hopes I am a sister, or half-sister. I see his disappointment when I state my name and tell him why I'm here. 'And you?' I ask. He says it, white as a sheet: 'I am a son.'

We introduce ourselves and exchange a bit of personal history. C. G. was two years old when he was placed in foster care; he has no memories of family life. At sixteen he paid a visit to his biological father. 'You're always curious about who he is, you think maybe he'll also… you never know.' The father opened the door and told him never to show his face there again. So C. never did face his father again. He is now 54 years young. 'And then came that form letter from the city of Amsterdam, that he – my father – was dead, and I thought: I'll go. But I won't tell them beforehand. If I can't manage it, then I won't go.'

He rights himself, motorcycle helmet in both hands, surrounded by the silence of St. Barbara. He managed it.

Meanwhile, Starik, also not a sibling, has arrived and

smokes a cigarette with C., who goes into the chapel to take pictures of the coffin. 'I've got that of him, at least.' He would like to say something during the service, he says when he returns. He does not yet know what. 'Something will come to you,' says the officiant. He nods. She does the same. We go outside.

After the first piece of music, a partita by Bach, C. walks forward. He looks at the coffin in silence for a while. Then he says in a firm voice: 'I don't know what to say,' falls silent again, and then, with difficulty: 'except that I loved you a lot,' turns toward the coffin, takes his time as he caresses the wood. Finally he gives it a sort of pat on the shoulder and returns to his seat. It is by far the most impressive speech I have ever heard.

I read out my thirty-two lines. A door must have blown open somewhere, for the paper flaps perilously. We listen to the second piece of music, Keith Jarrett, an excerpt from 'Testament', live in Paris, entirely improvised; occasionally a brief, intrinsic groan emerges from the music. After that (the officiant: 'We will now accompany Mr. W. G. to his final resting place. I ask you all to stand out of respect for his life') the last piece of music begins, again a Bach partita. The pallbearers have come forward with rustling footsteps, they've taken their place on either side of the coffin, have already bowed, the words 'Gentleman, if you please' have been spoken, when C. says: 'Can I ask something? I'd like to help carry him. May I?' He may, and between the others he walks alongside his father. Carry that load. Jacket fronts flap; left and right, trees are bursting into bud and bloom. 'He can't ever take this from me,' he will say later, in the coffee room. 'I did it the way *I* wanted to. I came, and he didn't send me away. He's not in charge any more.'

The courage to do it, without anaesthetic: cauterize a wound, and carry on living with a clean scar.

Starik takes a picture with C.'s cell phone as they lower the coffin into the grave. We all stand in silence at the green pit, we toss a handful of sand, we go to the coffee. On the way back, Starik's lighter won't ignite. His hands are shaking, but that's not it. It's windy.

FOR AN UNIMAGINABLE MAN

I've made an empty spot, with death its name.
I look at it from all sides, not a clue.
You are not there. Neither are you in me.

If from the centre someone started whistling
I might imagine what you sounded like,
so I invent a whistling and the grass

is getting up to hear it. I could well
carry a tone like that in my hand; it
would be as empty then as now, but I

would curl my fingers round that hollow, say
that I had got you, separate from all others,
then I'd let people take a look at you

and everyone would recognise this spot,
a place where someone is who is not there,
and realise that death does not exist,

nor emptiness. For what one cannot think
cannot exist. And if you should once more –

Though probably it's better emptiness,
an empty spot, exists and death's a spot
equally imaginable as one

you do not know could be, a dreamed-of house.
I think I would go out and into it
just like that tone inside and out of me:

it could be death exists if you go round
and round a sort of empty spot, one spot
is maybe all a person can imagine;

that something lives there, if need be just light
or darkness, or just emptiness, although
of that no man has knowledge. Dead one, I

stood behind your hedge, peeped through your window,
I thought I saw you in there but I saw
nothing, an empty spot to just exist.

Eva Gerlach, translated by John Irons

Mr. A. F. R.

Wednesday, 21 January 2015, 10:00 a.m.
St. Barbara Cemetery
Duty poet: Maria Barnas

Van Bokhoven phones on Friday afternoon, getting on for four o'clock, a time I feel one could safely call the beginning of the weekend. 'It concerns the discovery of a body,' he says without preamble. 'Yesterday evening.' He spells the name of the deceased. Born on 14 September 1947, died on 15 January 2015. 'Single, no children, both parents deceased. There is a sister who, after several serious operations, cannot walk or write, so is unable to attend the funeral.'

And even if she *were* able to attend, she would not. Because he had threatened to kill her. 'He was a schizophrenic.' She also knows with absolute certainty that he did not want to be cremated. So he will be buried. Moreover, she is convinced, he did it to himself. 'It was suicide.' The police have not commented on either 'fact', but the timely release of the body indicates a natural death.

Communicating with the sister is difficult. She cries incessantly through the telephone; she does not sound, to put it politely, entirely coherent. There is another sister, but there had been no contact with her for thirty years. She won't come either, Van Bokhoven presumes. He will check out the apartment on Monday; the keys are presently in the possession of the police.

On Monday morning Van Bokhoven rings again. There will be family there on Wednesday, after all. The other sister. With her husband, the deceased's brother-in-law, with whom he has had no contact either, these past thirty years. Perhaps a neighbour a few doors down, and a friend. 'But the assignment was made last Friday, so I'm not going to call it off.' He has not been to the apartment yet; he'll probably call me again at the end of the afternoon. There is still no official cause of death. But there is a chance it could have been carbon monoxide poisoning.

'Suddenly everybody's butting in,' he says, slightly put out. It also appears there is a feral cat living in Mr. R.'s backyard.

Do you know what music you want? I ask Maria. At first I considered 'The Dirt' by Mirel Wagner, but I don't dare, not with a few uncertain visitors in attendance. Maria does not respond to this, but does send me more questions.

'Has the cause of death been established yet? What does the estranged sister know about it? Or was it the no-sister who brought up poisoning? Why did the fire department go there on 15 January, "at full speed", according to the Internet?'

I suddenly realize I have totally forgotten to google Mr. R.

CO_2, I now read in the fire department's alarm report. That date coincides with the date the body was discovered. So he'll have been found by the firemen.

Maria has more questions. 'Do you know anything else about the cat? Did R. have a cat flap? Could the wild cat have been his? Can we ask Van Bokhoven?'

I call Van Bokhoven once more. 'Sorry,' I say. 'I'm entirely at your disposal,' he replies. Yes, there was a cat flap in the kitchen. The cat was – more or less – his. He had a friend who has a key to the house. The friend, together with Mentrum, the city psychiatric services, will see to it that a new home is found for the cat.

Wednesday comes. As I cycle through the park to the cemetery, a thin skin of ice has formed on the runnels and the grass has a light touch of frost. An evenly grey sky. Eight pallbearers are standing at the gate. New blood. They are still boys. Boys with meticulous haircuts. Boys without hats. Surely they'll put away their cell phones when the hearse pulls up? R. must have had good funeral insurance.

In the coffee room I meet the sister and her husband; we shake hands and they tell me they had hesitated, but this is, after all, one of those things you shouldn't let pass. I tell them I'm glad they came. The aide from Mentrum. The neighbour lady from down the road. And the friend, almost a neighbour, too. He talks a mile a minute, not always easy to follow. He is wearing a woollen cap with the number 666 on the back. I inquire about the cat. 'We were just talking about it,' he says. 'It's not like you can just catch him. He's really wild. Went inside now and again to eat, but then was off again. And say we do manage to catch him – what then? A shelter's no life for him. He's an outdoor animal. He won't want to be cooped up indoors.'

'No,' I agree. 'And they won't have an easy time finding him a new home, either.'

'Exactly. They'll end up putting him down.'

The neighbour says she lives on the second floor. 'Just throw food down to him, maybe?'

I ask if there are any specific music requests. 'Willy Alberti,' the friend suggests. 'Or Johnny Cash. But he never listened to music, not any more. Always had the TV on. Loud.' I go over to Mr. Degenkamp to see what we can do. We find a CD with Willy Alberti singing 'O beautiful Westertoren'. Hmm. And André Hazes: 'The Kite'. Might go down well, too. And we'll close with Andrea Bocelli: 'Panis Angelicus'. My plan is met with approval. 'Does anyone want to say a few words?' I ask. 'There's room for that, naturally. The duty poet will be there, she'll read a poem, but should any of you want to speak…' No. 'That won't be necessary,' the sister says, and her husband concurs, he wouldn't know what to say; only the friend says he thought about it on the way here, whether to say something, because there's plenty to tell, but where do you start? He shakes his head, presses his index fingers against his temples, and explains, 'I talk here. That's enough for me.'

I ask the officiant if he'll repeat the invitation after

the second piece of music. Maybe it'll help: having heard the poem; someone might feel moved to add something. Meanwhile, Maria has arrived. She hesitates. 'Should I really be doing this? I had so little to go on. Mainly just the cat.' I assure her it will be fine. The officiant wants to get started, but someone is using the toilet, and I know the brother-in-law needs to go, too, so we wait a bit.

The little group goes into the chapel, chatting animatedly while André Hazes sings. The friend is deep in conversation with the man from Mentrum, and behind us, too, the conversation continues. I glance at Maria, amused, and she too cracks a cautious smile. 'It feels like a café, what with the chitchat and the schlager music,' she whispers. And she's right, it sounds like the kind of Amsterdam brown café where Hazes was the standard background music. Maria has – so as to neither laugh nor cry – fixed her gaze on the chapel's wooden statue of the Virgin Mary, who is cradling not an infant but rather a kind of Lego construction.

When Hazes is finished, I glance back, wondering if the officiant will introduce Maria, but he nods that it's okay for her to go ahead, and I in turn nod to her. Suddenly it's quiet: the company watches her expectantly. She speaks from behind the lectern, softly but effectively.

LOOKING FOR YOU
   or A.F.R. (1947-2015)

The cat preferred to be outside.
I've had one like that too.

I was walking through the city and saw you
streets away from home. I called

but you acted as though you didn't know me.
Later I saw you looking for something in some shrubs.

The traffic was whirling in all directions.
I grabbed hold of you. Won't you come to me.

You scratched my face open
and then I saw that you weren't mine.

We don't listen. Don't answer.
No name no bowl no ties

round the neck with waterproof
address tag to restrain us.

Listen to the fearful bells peal out.
We will find repose

in how a wary creature beckons in us.
We won't get caught.

Maria Barnas, translated by Donald Gardner

   When she is finished, the friend vigorously nods with
approval. 'Yes. Beautiful. Thanks!' he says. For a moment it
looks as though he's going to stand up and hug the poet, but she

has already taken her seat. In the pew behind us, too, we hear appreciative mumbling. Willy Alberti sings of his beautiful Westertoren to the now-quiet chapel. Then the officiant comes forward to say we'll be paying our last respects shortly; he asks if anyone wants to say something, spreads his hands invitingly, an abashed 'no' comes from the pews. 'Well, there's always the chance to say something at the grave, if anyone so wishes.' Then he asks us to stand, out of respect for the deceased, as we listen to the last piece of music, after which we will head outside. It's a while before the pallbearers appear – let's hope they've turned off their cell phones – but there they are, the coffin is shouldered, we go outside.

Our modest cortège proceeds slowly. The lively chatting has resumed. As though nothing has happened.

When we reach the grave, the brother-in-law decides he wants to take a picture for the absent sister, so that she was kind of here, after all. But he's not sure how, or his camera refuses to function. I offer to do it, take out my mobile phone. The man from Mentrum does the same. Then we can just e-mail the photos, right? On this, we agree. We fumble self-consciously with our cameras – it's a wonder any pictures were taken all.

Good, everyone's been photographed – well, he's not in his, and I'm not in mine. The coffin is lowered. The friend takes out two bunches of roses, one white and one light-red, and wriggles two flowers out, tosses them onto the coffin. The officiant takes over: he deftly removes the rubber band from the stems, loosens the bunches and offers the remaining mourners two flowers each, one white, one red. Careful, he says, hold it down at the bottom, and he points to the thorns, very thoughtful.

We each toss two flowers. There are exactly enough flowers: at least something tallies. There is coffee, there will be coffee. We talk about the cat, about how we won't get caught. Maria says she did, in fact, own a half-wild cat – well, own, you can't own an animal – a cat she took with her to Berlin and which ran away, because it was used to having a yard, and refused to be cooped up all day. He sat inside for weeks, who knows, maybe months, yowling piteously until he grabbed his chance and escaped. Months later she saw him again, a few blocks from her house. She called to him, but he pretended not to recognize her – which in the poem turned out to be true.

Maria offers the officiant a copy of her poem, to put into the folder where he's collected documents relating to the R. case. He looks at her as though she's offered him another helping of beans, and doesn't want to hurt her feelings: 'No... that's not really necessary.'

Afterwards Maria says she might have been a bit too outspoken with the sister, who had come after all but didn't really know why, because she and her brother hadn't seen each other in thirty years. Maria had spelt it out for her: 'If you don't go, then you can spend the rest of your life regretting not going, but if you do go, the worst that can happen is that you regret having wasted that one day.' He was a few years younger than she, said the sister. As children, they had been close. Later, things happened that were out of his control. Psychological problems.

No one – the sister, the neighbours, the family, nor the man from Mentrum – knew anything about carbon monoxide poisoning. So the CO_2 theory was immediately off the table. No, he had a weak heart. Yes, everyone concurred. It wouldn't take much to bring that heart of his to a standstill. And he was also starting to lose his memory. He'd telephone with the remote control, or operate the TV with his phone.

Just before he leaves, the friend says he thought the cat poem was just the ticket. 'He loved animals. Sometimes he'd spend all day in his backyard with the toads and snakes. He was a special man. There was something remarkable about him.'

I bring up Younger Brother's cat, the cat who was nicknamed 'Little Cow' because her markings resembled those of a Friesian cow. One day she, too, just ran off. Years later, Little Cow was spotted behind the window of a house across the street, by all appearances entirely at home with her new family, simply in a new life somewhere else.

Not here.

Mr. M. N. P.

Born 3 March 1941 in Lousame, Spain, died in
Stuivenberg Hospital, Antwerp, 29 September 2010.
Monday 11 October 2010, Schoonselhof Cemetery
Duty poet: Stijn Vranken

On the Internet, M.N.P. is the Secretary-general of a council of guilds, a young competitive surfer, a celebrated soldier, a lawyer, and a cheerful 22-year-old with forty-eight Facebook friends, but on this splendid autumn day in October at Schoonselhof Cemetery, Mr. M.N.P. is most of all a stranger. Renée, from the Firm, informed me of Mr. M.N.P.'s lonely funeral, as neither the police nor civil registry had come up with any next of kin.

Mr. M.N.P. lived in Antwerp, in the Seefhoek quarter, close to Stuivenberg Hospital where he passed away, in poet Stijn Vranken's neighbourhood. Little else is known about him. The Internet reveals that M.N.P. is a common name in Spain, but a search in combination with his birthplace yields 'no results'. When I phone the hospital for more information I am put on hold, then transferred to the Intensive Care Unit, where they summon the doctor who last tended Mr. M.N.P.

There is a bit of confusion. The name on the patient's dossier in the doctor's possession differs from the surname I was given by a single letter, but the doctor and I conclude that it concerns one and the same person. A female friend had been present when Mr. M.N.P. was admitted, the doctor tells me. A Brazilian, she guesses, because she thought the woman spoke Portuguese. Perhaps she was Spanish, I suggest to myself. The friend had discovered Mr. M.N.P. two days earlier sitting in his easy chair, in what she presumed was a state of inebriation, and had left him there to sweat out the hangover. When there was no word two days later, she returned to have a another look, and when Mr. M.N.P. still did not respond, she called for an ambulance. Mr. M.N.P. died that same day in the hospital from a severe stroke. There was little anyone could do for him.

The language barrier prevented the hospital from informing the friend about what came next, about the fate of Mr. M.N.P.'s remains and when the funeral would take place. The doctor advises me to call the mortuary, because Mr. M.N.P.'s friend had gone there to pay her respects, and might have left her name and number. Then there would be no need for a lonely funeral.

In vain. The staff member at the morgue does recall the Brazilian friend, but says she came to pay her very last respects, and did not leave any contact information. Mr. M.N.P. might have a wife and child back in Spain, the hospital employee suggests, but they would have been notified by the police or the hospital. Precisely who informed whom, he can't recall.

Who knows what Mr. M.N.P. kept secret. That a wife and child might suddenly surface strikes me as unlikely: for all we know, they don't exist, seeing as the civil registry had no record of any family.

Here in the golden sunlight, on what promises to be a fine autumn day, there is not a soul in sight, except for a few pallbearers having one last quick cigarette. Although there is no smoking in the procession or near the grave, they burn through a lot of tobacco in the moments before and after. It shortens the wait, gives one something to do. One of the youngest pallbearers tells me this is his last week in this autumn chill: he has lost his heart to Jamaica and will be heading there within the week. Fourteen hours in the air, plus a one-hour stop, during which he will no doubt light up a few cigarettes in the smoking lounge. It's warm there, he says, not too warm, just warm. Comfy-warm. I look at the fog banks that hover above the plots, and shiver in my lightweight blazer. I make a mental note to get myself a heavier suit before winter comes.

When Stijn Vranken arrives, he offers me a lift with him out to Section U, where the coffin is lifted onto the shoulders and we walk the short distance to the grave. Soon after the coffin is placed on the trestles, Stijn is given the sign that he can proceed, and I realize too late that the two pots of purple heather I brought with me are still on the ground beside the grave rather than on top of the coffin, as is our routine. Too late, but no matter; the heather will simply get planted at the head of the grave, once it has been filled, next to the marker with the gracefully lettered name.

THIS COULD HAVE BEEN A SONG

There is a hole. A box. A name.
No doubt at all: there was a life.

That means there was a birth, and growth,
desire, there was love, a wife, a child
is officially suspected. Somewhere in Spain.

There is no doubt. This could have been a song.

There was a break-up, someone left, swapping more
for less again and again. There were disappearances,
one step further each time. To here: Seefhoek, Antwerp.

This could have been a song.
This is wind. Some words beneath
a feeble sun and no way back.

This could have been a song.

Stijn Vranken, translated by David Colmer

After paying our respects to Mr. M.N.P., we take leave of the young officiant. We say goodbye – but not for long: two hours later, at twelve noon, we'll see each other again at the entrance to Schoonselhof Cemetery for the next lonely funeral, for Mr. A.D.S.

Later this afternoon there was supposed to be yet another one, the funeral of Mr. L.V.H., but I respectfully turned that one down. I was able to contact the nursing home where Mr. L.V.H. had passed away, and a few staff members in his unit spontaneously offered to attend his funeral, so at the last moment there was someone to see him off after all. Two lonely funerals in a single day, down from three. Still two too many, I sigh.

Mr. Nguyen Van Kham

Born 1 September 1954 in Thakhek, Laos and found in
his apartment in Antwerp 4 November 2010.
He had, it is believed, already been dead for two years.
Tuesday, 16 November 2010, Schoonselhof Cemetery
Duty poet: Maarten Inghels

Never before had Mr. Nguyen Van Kham received
so much attention – and so long after his death at that.
Having sent, to no avail, repeated demands for back rent,
the collection officer knocked on his door on 4 November
and discovered Mr. Nguyen Van Kham's mummified body.
At that point Nguyen Van Kham had been dead for nearly
two years. The neighbours recall an unpleasant smell in
the corridor, but eventually it had receded and life just
continued blithely on its way. Only when the collection
officer, arrears accounts in hand, got no answer, did anyone
wonder why.

The 54-year-old boat refugee becomes a news item on
television and in the papers; the discussion of his death
continues later that evening in a nightly current affairs
programme, after which they broadcast a short film about
'urban loneliness'. A coroner tells us how a corpse can
become naturally mummified. The neighbours declare
their complete ignorance of the situation. Every news item
includes a word from a social worker, whose task it is to
promote contact amongst residents of housing projects.
For instance, the residents of two blocks of flats facing
each other have agreed to open their curtains when they
wake up, so people will know if something's amiss with
the neighbours across the way.

On the late news I see Paula, a volunteer at Kamiano[6] after a memorial service for Mr. Nguyen Van Kham. She calls on all of us to show more solidarity, to be better neighbours. People gather at the apartment in Block 444, erected out of soulless concrete, to lay flowers in the doorway. Candles are lit.

The next day's newspaper quotes one neighbour, Jenny, as recalling Mr. Nguyen Van Kham as well groomed, always impeccably dressed. But because of the language difference, she admits, they had no social contact. No getting together for a coffee or dropping by the other's flat. Mr. Nguyen lived on the fourth floor and had it to himself for many years; she lived three flights down. They passed each other in the stairwell sometimes, yes, a friendly, nice-looking man. Even cleaned up other people's rubbish in the hallway.

Says she hadn't seen him in a while, assumed he was on vacation in some far-flung corner of the world, or had had an accident and was recuperating, or had suddenly moved out, without anyone taking his place. She did sort his mail, separating the personal post from the junk mail, and kept it in neat stacks. He'll turn up again, she thought. What will happen to those stacks of mail now I don't know. If no one notices you when you're alive, they won't when you're dead either.

Before I take tram 24 out to Schoonselhof Cemetery, I have to polish my shoes for Mr. Nguyen Van Kham. Yesterday I was at Schoonselhof too, to visit the graves of all the lonely funerals. On top Mr. A.D.S.'s grave, the last one in the row, was a mountain of floral arrangements, roses, and wreaths. But there had been no one at his funeral. I was curious to see who took such great interest in him after his death, who placed all those flowers, whence this noble gesture.

[6] An Antwerp restaurant for the homeless.

As I set out to walk past the flowers, between Mr. A.D.S. and Mr. M.N.P.'s graves, to get to the head end with the simple nameplate, I sank into a patch of soggy earth masquerading as solid ground, up to my ankles in mud, and had to extricate myself rather inelegantly. Once back on dry land, I was able to read the ribbon attached to one of the wreaths: it was from 'dos amigos', his Spanish friends who could not be reached before the funeral. I forgot about my shoes, I was glad that Mr. A.D.S. had received more honours then we had initially expected.

I arrive at the main entrance of the cemetery, in clean shoes, for the funeral of Mr. Nguyen Van Kham, and greet Bert. Twenty people have already gathered in a small cluster, an unexpected band of sympathizers of all sizes, ages, and colours. A bright layer of mist hangs low over the graves, you can't see very far, the light is ghostly white. It's not long before the first two photographers sneak into Schoonselfhof; later, a few more will appear, in the company of a journalist. Two newspapers and public television have come to report on Mr. Nguyen Van Kham's last send-off, as though in life he had been an international celebrity. The group waiting for the funeral has now grown to thirty – a stark contrast with the other lonely funerals, where it is usually dead quiet.

I greet Paula, who has come to show her support, and has brought red roses to distribute among those present. She hasn't got enough. Flowers and wreaths, together with my two potted heather plants, are put into the hearse, on top of the coffin. Paula informs me that the Asian-looking visitors used to be friendly with Mr. Nguyen; they've brought along photos from the old days. Nevertheless they did not speak one another's language. Together with some Vietnamese and fellow Laotians, Mr. Nguyen had lived in a Red Cross refugee centre in Merksem in the mid-1990s. Back then he worked as a tailor in Aartselaar, where he took in and let out men's suits. Later, apparently, Mr. Nguyen and his colleagues had a falling-out. Contact was broken, resolutely and long-term. Nguyen Van Kham retreated into his home, and seldom went out.

Later I would read in the newspaper that Nguyen Van Kham did celebrate in company, one last time. His neighbour Saidi, an older Moroccan musician, invites him for a meal and a bottle of whisky on New Year's Eve 2007. The conversation does not really get off the ground, seeing as both gentlemen only speak a few words of broken Dutch. Saidi takes out his acoustic guitar, and Nguyen Van Kham whistles along. Red wine flows, they laugh, make music, and say goodbye in the early hours of the morning.

Nguyen Van Kham's former acquaintances take out a camera and photograph one another in various poses in front of the hearse, the coffin, and, later, the grave. When the procession starts moving, the press photographers swarm like paparazzi around the motley gathering. They constantly tread on the grass, jog thirty feet ahead and then turn to snap pictures of the mourners.

When we arrive at Section U, the pallbearers first carry all the flower arrangements to the grave. The group waits obediently, a mobile phone rings and its owner answers loudly, after which we follow the coffin to the grave. Once it has been placed on trestles, and the murmur has subsided, Bert thanks those present for attending, and gives me a sign that I can precede with the poem for Nguyen Van Kham. I falter occasionally as I read it, and my legs tremble. All the while, a microphone is shoved under my nose.

THIS MUCH ATTENTION

The Mekong River was a seam between
your hometown and another no-man's-land,
and yet your journey's end
was edged by even more unknowns.

Your bank statements in hand,
we assume you lived among us,
fourth floor, in a bygone calendar year,
a friendly man, well-groomed, alone.

You fell ill, lay beside your bed,
your back turned on life; while the process
had vexed generations of Egyptians,
you became a mummy all on your own.

Seven minutes on prime-time news,
your demise dissected on evening TV,
a column on page two of the paper –
This much attention, you've never been shown.

Uneasy with your passing, indignation
suddenly makes us better neighbours:
Jenny downstairs would have liked a coffee
if only she spoke your native tongue.

We failed, I freely confess, only
noticing you when your money dried up.
Two dead years you held your peace, yet
who you are, we should have known.

Maarten Inghels, translated by Jonathan Reeder

    After reading out the poem, I lay it on top of the coffin,
so it can be buried along with him. Officiant Bert gives a
sign that everyone may now pay their last respects. The
Asian group is clearly troubled by Mr. Nguyen's bizarre
departure. Halfway through the line of mourners, it is the
turn of Jenny, the downstairs neighbour. For me she was
just a name in the newspaper, now she suddenly appears
before me in real life.

Wearing a blue anorak, she strides forward and takes a handwritten letter from her inside pocket. She motions to Bert that she would like to speak, to read something out, a few words she has prepared. She launches into her speech with an assertive 'Dearest Neighbour', after which she unleashes an editorial sermon: 'My speech might not be original, but you can't stress enough that in a society that's only interested in money, it's not so strange that a person can lie dead in his flat for two years. As long as you pay your bills, they leave you alone. But the minute the cash register stops ringing, they come after you. [...] We, the neighbours, couldn't do anything, they don't listen to us anyway. We found that out last year. We're still waiting for answers to questions about wrongful charges. Unfortunately, *we* can't send around a collection officer. Yes, neighbour, I hope you've gone to a truly socially-minded place. Because you'll have learned one thing about getting older: humanity, solidarity, and honesty don't make you rich. Bye, neighbour.'

I think of Thakhek in Laos, southeast Asia. I've never been, but with the help of Google Maps I've tried to put together a picture for myself of the place where Mr. Nguyen Van Kham grew up, in a small house on Main Road, a key thoroughfare leading to the Mekong River. One of Asia's mightiest rivers, over which, at the age of twenty-one, Mr. Nguyen crossed into Thailand before ending up in foreign, cold Belgium.

After everyone has had the chance to pay their last respects in their own way, the coffin is lowered, to the flashing of cameras. Then the company crumbles apart, the media asks various mourners a few more questions, and then everyone returns homeward, on foot or by car, in the mist that hangs over the cemetery like a heavy veil.

Mr. L. L.

Born 9 August 1938 in Kapellen,
found in his Antwerp apartment on 11 February 2011.
Monday 21 February 2011, Schoonselfhof Cemetery
Duty poet: Jan Aelberts

'WOMAN, 72, LOCKED IN HOUSE FOR THREE WEEKS WITH HUSBAND'S BODY', reads the front-page headline of the tabloid *Gazet van Antwerpen* on 15 February. I'm standing in a deli and turn to page two, where the backstory is allotted a full page. The wife suffers from dementia, and was locked in her apartment with the body of her dead husband for more than three weeks. Accompanying the article is a photograph of the apartment building, one of those large housing projects one finds on the fringes of Antwerp. I assume this will not mean a lonely funeral. The man, after all, had a wife named Celine, according to the paper, and that evening's television news item features statements by various concerned neighbours.

And yet a few days later I receive an e-mail from Renée saying that Mr. L.L., known to the neighbours as 'Lou', will be given a civil funeral, thanks to the intervention of the Antwerp social services. In the e-mail, his wife is suddenly no longer named Celine, but Martha. I ask Renée if Mr. L.L.'s wife, despite her illness, might still attend the funeral, or whether anyone has come forward as next of kin, but the answer is short and sweet: no one has shown interest in being present at the funeral.

Later, it occurs to me that a woman whose dementia is so advanced that she does not realize her husband has been dead for three weeks would see no need to grieve at his grave. I wonder where Celine or Martha is now, what's going through her head, whether, in a lucid moment, she still thinks of Lou.

I retrieve the newspaper article from the archives. The tragic story came to light after concerned neighbours broke down the door to the apartment. They had heard knocking at night, but did not realize it was the woman trying to attract attention. One neighbour says he rang their bell once, but that the wife shouted back that she couldn't get the door open. The neighbour assumed everything was in order, and added that after all, it was Lou, not the wife, with whom he chatted at the mailboxes. The main reason she never left the apartment was because a special lock on the front door prevented the senile woman from wandering off on her own. The police were called in and performed the necessary lab work at the scene, a spokesman said, but nothing whatsoever indicated foul play. It was, he stresses, a tragic incident.

I wonder how the woman managed to survive those last weeks. The shopping trolley full of groceries stood untouched in the front hall, and there was no indication that she had eaten anything. When the neighbours broke down the door, she was completely ignorant of what had happened, and kept talking about a doll in the bedroom, without realizing it was her husband who lay next to the bed.

I send a message to Jan Aelberts, asking if he is available to write a suitable poem for Mr. L.L. Later I'll send him the relevant news articles, adding that Lou's sole hobby was repairing old computers. But most of his time was devoted to caring for his wife – they were inseparable. The old computers were kept in the basement storage room, but thieves stole them all a week after his death.

I buy three heather plants, white this time, and make my way to Schoonselhof Cemetery, where a van from the Firm is already parked. Two pallbearers are keeping warm inside, they nod to me. A florid red rose is stencilled on the side of the van. I'm half an hour early, but soon enough Bert's small white car pulls up. He says I can wait with him in the car, until the corpse arrives.

'I can say that, right? Corpse?' he asks. 'Some people might find that disrespectful, but that is what it's called, isn't it.' A few minutes later the hearse arrives and now we only have to wait for Jan, who has called to say his train is delayed. Bert tells me what he did prior to his job as officiant for the Firm. He used to be affiliated with the Norbertine monks, and later worked in a parish in Antwerp for a priest who is now a candidate for bishop.

'He's more along the lines of Archbishop Léonard,' Bert says. 'That doesn't really do it for me.'

'Conservative,' I remark.

'Traditionally-minded,' he says. 'They prefer to call it traditionally-minded.'

The dashboard clock reads 13:58. Jan walks through the entrance gate.

'Right on time,' Bert says. Jan gets in and we drive to the designated section. There, the coffin is lifted onto four shoulders and carried to the grave, where it is placed on trestles. Bert gives the sign that Jan can read out his poem.

* * *

She spoke of a doll in the bedroom, a one-way ticket
back to childhood. Understanding floated off like a tower block
in the clouds. The shadow of the first parachutist
fell on the city. He left your body cold.

For twenty days no rescue came.
Life went on as in a doll's house where there is no death
and everyone's asleep, where hope can kiss
us all awake, a prophet on slack strings.

She knocked on the walls until they found you,
next to her. They put it in the paper.
She spoke of a doll in the bedroom, a one-way ticket.

Jan Aelberts, translated by David Colmer

The graveyard is completely quiet, and a bitingly cold
wind whips against our cheeks. The weatherman predicted
that this would be the last winter sting, that spring should
kick in next week. Bert indicates that we can now pay our
respects and shows us how, as though it's our first time.
Then the coffin is lowered and Bert says we can bow our
heads one more time at the grave, which we do. That extra
bow is new, I think to myself. It breaks the routine.

Afterwards, we shake hands with the pallbearers and
Bert writes his telephone number on a slip of paper. 'Might
come in handy,' he says. On the back of the paper are details
of the next funeral, which Bert and the pallbearers hurry
off to perform. Under 'remarks' is written: 'Light classical
music.'

'Vivaldi,' says Bert. 'The Four Seasons.'

ANTWERP
LONELY FUNERAL NO. 20

Mr. R. G.

Born 10 August 1956 in Merksem, died 25 November 2011.
Thursday 8 December 2011, Schoonselhof Cemetery
Duty poet: Andy Fierens

On Monday morning, 5 December, I receive a message from Renée that, after a long hiatus, there will be another lonely funeral. Police have found Mr. R.G. in his apartment. He was unmarried. The e-mail closes, as usual, with 'no further details known'.

After replying that poet Andy Fierens will write a poem and attend the funeral, I am given the telephone number of the chief of police, and the number of the dossier he has drawn up. Monday, however, is the chief's day off, I'm told. And officially, confidentiality regulations prohibit him from divulging information about Mr. R.G., or about anyone else.

I had hoped for a bit more information about Mr. R.G. How long had he been dead, were there any photographs, did he have any hobbies? The duty detective promises to relay my request to his superior, and advises me to petition the law courts for access to the dossier. But there, too, I come away empty-handed. You have to make a request in writing, and authorization from the public prosecutor can take up to five working days.

Personal traits, even just a few, would be handy in composing the poem, but on the other hand, I don't know if I want to know all the details of Mr. R.G.'s death. I believe there is a limit on how far one can delve into another person's life, but where that boundary lies is not always evident.

I decide to cycle over to the home of the unfortunate Mr. R.G. There might be neighbours who noticed his sudden

115

disappearance. On Google Street View, the app that allows you to wander the streets of a city at your computer screen, I type in the address, and a pair of apartment blocks appear. From the house number I deduce that R.G. lived on the fourth floor, but when I try to scroll upwards, the building becomes blurry. The Google camera apparently does not film vertically. A Moroccan woman in a black hijab pushes a pram along the pavement in front of the building. She looks directly into the lens, but her face has been blurred. That's one of the Google rules – we mustn't be able to recognize anyone.

Perhaps Mr. R.G. was also walking around somewhere as Google's car drove through Antwerp; maybe he was filmed while taking a stroll around the block or on his way to the shops, immortalized on a screen-shot, with the street as decor. I know, for instance, that if I type in my parents' address, I'll see a woman with a pixellated face bending over to empty the mailbox. I know it is my mother, because no perfect stranger would be emptying my parents' mailbox. But I can hardly scroll up and down every street in Antwerp on Google Street View in search of Mr. R.G., not least because I don't know what he looks like.

The city of Antwerp swells out in all directions, flows from urban to suburban and from city centre to harbour, interrupted only by the occasional highway or the Schelde. Today's destination is the last street before the city ends. The street is not much more than a parking lot with a collection of rubbish bins and a pair of high-rise apartment blocks. It is an appendix of the city – you could easily overlook it, or snip it off. Nothing but fields behind the apartment blocks, a grassy space on ground once polluted by oil refineries where festivals are now held in summertime.

When I arrive, the Moroccan woman with the hijab is, of course, no longer walking past the building. Plenty of other women are, though, all of them pushing pushchairs or dragging whining children by the hand. If I peer through the opening of Mr. R.G.'s mailbox I can see a department store leaflet on the top of the pile. After ringing three different neighbours' bells, the fourth one answers. Yes, the lady knew that Mr. R.G. had passed away. 'Wait,' she says through the intercom, 'I'll come down.'

The neighbour maintains a distance of two metres. Every time I move closer, she shrinks further back. She's pushing sixty, I reckon.

'He died.'

'You didn't know him?' I ask.

'Nah, he kept himself to himself,' she replies.

'But didn't you ever talk to him?'

'No, he was a recluse. The cleaning lady came once a week, and one day there was no answer. So they called Social Services and the police. They found him in bed,' the neighbour says. 'He had probably died the previous day.'

That's all I find out. The police chief calls me that evening having received my message. He kindly explains that Mr. R.G. did not have many possessions, just a table, a couple of chairs, an armchair, and a bed. He can't tell me much else, but says he'll be returning to the apartment next week, this time accompanied by the civil magistrate. But that is too late for me.

On the day of the funeral, Andy and I go to the block of flats. 'Woonhaven'—that's the social housing service – is located on the ground floor. They must have known Mr. R.G. There are more than thirty people waiting, but we're able to corner a staff member who is just leaving the office. He gives us the number of Mr. R.G.'s contact person at Social Services, but he can only remember having arranged a social housing flat for Mr. R.G. because his previous apartment was derelict, and that he helped him move. After that, contact between R.G. and Social Services was negligible.

After all that trouble, Andy and I still know precious little about Mr. R.G., other than that he led a sober life and had moved into social housing, only to die there without ever receiving a visitor. He will be buried on Thursday morning, 8 December. It's still dark when I leave home and arrive at Schoonselhof just before nine. Andy is there already. The mood is jolly at the entrance to the cemetery. The first pallbearer to get out of the van is new to me. He has a white chinstrap beard, meticulously trimmed. He tells me there aren't enough men to carry the coffin.

'So we've got a little problem,' he says. 'Our fellow was on the heavy side.'

'What about Andy and me?'

'That could work. Four pallbearers plus you two makes six. That should about do it.' Then the hearse carrying the coffin pulls up. Is it my imagination, or is the back end of the vehicle sagging?

'The smaller of you two can ride with the hearse, and the other one in the van.' Without a word, we take our respective positions. When I slide alongside the other two pallbearers in the front seat, I realize this is my first time in a hearse.

'Sitting up front's not so bad,' the pallbearer with the chinstrap beard says matter-of-factly. 'It's in back that you've got a problem.' But up front is pretty cramped as well, leg-wise. Two gravediggers are already there when we reach the plot. One of them fetches the dolly parked discreetly behind a hedge. Lifting the coffin is hard work, and it makes its way, with much ado, onto the dolly.

After the dolly has reached the grave cut, the men first work out a plan to get the coffin onto the trestles. Then there is time to read the poem and rest the arms before lowering the coffin into its final resting place. When the pallbearers and gravediggers initiate this risky undertaking, Andy darts forward to assist. My three white roses in cellophane wrapping are placed on the coffin.

ISOLATED, ABANDONED AND ALONE

They couldn't tell me much. I think of you
as a Crusoe who survived the shipwreck of his life
and stranded in a flat in Antwerp. Friday
was your cleaning lady. And other than that, no one.

55 years reduced to a single staggering second
that's come adrift of time in the ship of his coffin.

What can *I* do now? I have nothing to offer you.
Unless perhaps – what if I dream you up a different life,
another chance. Imagining improvements here and there,
it's what we do.

Thinking to myself, for instance: if I were your father,
I'd take you on my lap. As a friend, I'd give you
a shoulder. A wife, my faithful mouth.

Who would you like to be? How many chances do people need?
One? Ten? I don't have to see a photo to know what it was like,
an island six flights up, and all your own. A childhood dream.
But in the grown-up world that means isolated, abandoned
and alone.

'Where are you going?' I'll ask if I see you sailing by
when I am pitching on a thought or drifting
through a sleepless night. Then hitch a little ride.

Andy Fierens, translated by David Colmer

One of the gravediggers wipes a gloved finger over his eye, and remarks how moving the poem was. We nod in agreement, but our thoughts are mostly on Mr. R. G. and his unexpected girth. Getting an oversized coffin on trestles is one thing, but lowering it by two thin woven straps is quite another. But we managed. We bow our heads one last time for Mr. R.G. before we leave the grave.

The chinstrapped pallbearer recalls the time his black humour got him into trouble: 'I had gone to the morgue to pick up the body. Behind me, in the doorway, were three young nurses who didn't dare come in. The man on the table was so obese that I joked that they could have at least deflated him first, like a balloon.' His colleagues laugh. It's not the first time they've heard this anecdote.

'But the nurses were so shocked that they complained to the hospital management, and there was a bit of a fuss.' I can't help chuckling.

'Nothing wrong with humour,' I say. Sometimes, at the grave, hanging around the coffin, humour gets the upper hand. In this business, black humour is a way of letting off steam, and in the coffee room, too, one laughs as much as cries. Death must be relieved of its unforgiving harshness, and what better way than with a joke or an anecdote?

I am invited to squeeze back into the hearse for a lift to the cemetery gates. Our knees buckled, the chinstrap resumes his chronicle on burying 'special sizes'.

'A body that's been put in the freezer,' he says, 'sometimes doesn't fit in the coffin anymore.'

'Freezer?' I ask. I only know about the cooler.

'Once a body starts to decompose, it has to go into the freezer. But if the arm is bent, then the elbow sticks out too far and it won't go into the coffin. And then – just because the elbow sticks out and the body is frozen solid – we have to resort to special coffin sizes.'

'I never knew that,' I reply.

'Sometimes we ask them to tie the limbs down before the body goes into the freezer, so that nothing juts out.

Then you can just slide them out of the freezer and, bam, into the coffin.' When we arrive at the gate, I can just say I won't be at the next funeral before they rush off. 'See you next time,' they say. And: 'Thanks.'

Mr. H. H.

Born 7 January 1950 in Antwerp, died 25 May 2012.
Wednesday, 13 June 2012, Schoonselhof Cemetery
Duty poet: Stijn Vranken

Mr. H.H. still has family. There is a Mrs. H.H., but she does not wish to attend. She also has mobility problems, but the first reason is the primary one. I ask Renée if the wife would be prepared to speak to me: she might tell us something about her husband, share his life story, which always helps make the poem more personal. Renée replies that the woman was married to Mr. H.H. only on paper, and that they saw very little of each other—'it's a touchy subject'. So we will leave Mrs. H.H. in peace.

Mr. H.H. lived in Stijn Franken's neighbourhood, practically around the corner. H.H. died in Stuivenberg Hospital, likewise around the corner, so these circumstances make Stijn a suitable poet to compose something for him.

Since we know so little about Mr. H.H., I turn to Google. The combination of name and address produces, surprisingly enough, an almost immediate hit: a not-so-rosy picture of Mr. H.H., in the form of a newspaper clipping from the *Belgische Staatsblad*. It is a ruling by the civil magistrate of the Antwerp First District court, in which 'by power of the verdict of the Justice of the Peace, issued on 16 March 2012, Mr. H.H. shall be committed to Stuivenberg Hospital, judged to be incapable of managing his own affairs. Power of Attorney is hereby assigned to J.E., Solicitor, Antwerp.'

I forward the ruling, so recently appended to the civil registry, to Stijn. He suggests that the cause might have been dementia, adding that 'we're not so well designed, after all, we humans.' Placing someone under custody, or otherwise denying them freedom of movement, can also be required in the case of psychiatric problems, or a drinking problem, or any number of other reasons, but we resolve not to jump to conclusions or speculate on Mr. H.H.'s last months. Since we don't know, we let H.H.'s life rest simply upon an address, a hospital, his name.

'I've eased up this past year,' Stijn says. 'I get less worked up about the person's circumstances.'

The fact that we cannot speculate is confirmed when I see a cluster of people as I walk into Schoonselhof Cemetery carrying a pot of white daisies. There's a dog too – a golden retriever, I'm guessing, but my knowledge of dogs is limited. Family, after all: nine individuals who introduce themselves as mother, stepmother, sister, stepbrother, nephew and various other kin or in-laws. The organogram of blood relations is difficult to piece together.

I introduce myself and explain my purpose, and say that another poet is on his way, who has written something for Mr. H.H., that in this sense it is a lonely funeral, no matter how unwelcome those words might sound to the hastily assembled family members.

'I know about the project,' says the sister, or the mother, I'm not entirely sure. 'Who's paying for this poet, then?' I reassure her that the poet won't cost her anything, but that I do need her permission, otherwise the poet will keep quiet.

'I've heard of you people,' she continues. 'A colleague of mine read about it in the paper and said we should ask you, but I didn't know who to call.' I find it oddly contradictory that a family member would want to engage us for a funeral, but there's a first time for everything. She explains that H.H. was definitely lonely, that his wife wanted nothing to do with him – followed by several invectives directed at the wife – and that she never saw him.

'His wife sent word that the funeral would take place last Saturday at ten o'clock at Silsburg Cemetery,' the stepbrother says. 'We didn't believe her, but we went, just to be on the safe side. There was nothing.'

'She also said death announcements would be sent, but that never happened either. We've spent the last two weeks tracking down this funeral,' says the mother or sister. 'We only found out about it the day before yesterday.' So it's not a lonely funeral, I think to myself, but the family gives poet Stijn Vranken permission anyway. They even think it's a good idea 'that something gets said'. Stijn arrives, there's another round of hand-shaking, the dog cavorts while the family tells us about H.H. – apparently they have a lot to get off their chests. Mr. H.H. has three children too, they live somewhere in Limburg, far away; they had maintained contact with one another, but not with their father.

The people from the Firm are late; they are stuck in traffic. Two accidents in the city centre have caused traffic jams all the way to the periphery. Half an hour later than planned, the modern hearse pulls into Schoonselhof. We walk in procession behind the vehicle toward Section W1. A man approaches and asks who is being buried, but it appears he's here for a different funeral. At W1 I notice that the coffin being hoisted onto the shoulders is an oversized one.

Once the coffin, with my daisies on top, is resting on the trestle, a gust of wind blows, and Etienne signals to Stijn that he may proceed.

THIRTEEN QUESTIONS AND NO ANSWER

What have you got to lose?

Time? The dream that settles
in our heads as a cloud of proteins?
The past that doesn't exist?

What have you got to lose?

Light? My expression in your eyes?
The chance of a reunion? The future
we can't even remember anymore?

What did we ever have?

Eternity? Or just the question?
Is everything more fleeting
than ever ours?

Stijn Vranken, translated by David Colmer

One by one, we pay our last respects, ending with Stijn
and me. The dog is gone, maybe he's in the car. I cast a
glance at the graves of the previous two lonely funerals.
My flowers have been removed, or were never planted. We
take our leave of the family, express our condolences once
again – but they are preoccupied with collecting the papers
letting them off work today – and walk towards the exit.

Mr. G. D.

Born 29 April 1936 in Ledeberg, found dead in his
apartment 25 January 2013.
Tuesday, 12 February 2013, Schoonselhof Cemetery
Duty poet: Bernard Dewulf

I remember it well, the report on the *Gazet van Antwerpen* website. Later, I read the full article in the newspaper itself, about a man, found dead in his apartment near Stuivenberg Hospital, who had been entirely devoured by rats. All that was left was a skeleton. 'In my entire career, I've never seen anything like this,' the coroner was quoted. 'The plague could have broken out,' said the Disaster Victim Identity team from the national police. While he was alive, the man had kept a few pet rats in a cage, but after his death they had reproduced so prolifically that police 'had to kick dozens of them off the body.' The journalist wrote that the man had 'fallen prey' to rats. In the space of a week, his body was gone.

It's not often that I read about a death in the newspaper and think: I'll bet this means a lonely funeral. We had the homeless man who had fallen asleep on a park bench and never woke up (five lines in the newspaper), the mummified Vietnamese man (lots of newspaper articles, items on national television), and now there is the 'rat man', as he is popularly known. Sensational news that gives people the shivers, and makes them shake their heads in disbelief, especially at the words 'in an advanced state of decomposition'.

The *Gazet*'s coverage includes a side story listing previous cases of 'lonely deaths'. A woman in Zagreb is estimated to have sat dead in her easy chair for 22 years with the television on – neighbours thought she had moved house. And then there was the man from the hamlet of Minnertsga in Friesland, who lay rotting under a drafty attic window for four years. He shared a house with his two sisters and two brothers. One evening after dinner, he retired to his room with the words: 'I'm going upstairs, don't disturb me.' His siblings faithfully respected his wish.

The 'rat man' has a much nicer name: Mr. G.D., and he is the third elderly person we have buried this year. Or, rather: whose ashes we have scattered. His remains were transferred to a military hospital in Neder-Over-Heembeek to ascertain the cause and approximate time of death. The conclusion 'of natural causes' was reached later that week, whereupon his remains were cremated. I send Bernard Dewulf Mr. G.D.'s vital information, and he will write a poem. Little more is known than his name, his age – 71 years – and the story of the rats. Renée from the Firm informs me that the press may show up, due to previous media coverage. She says it would be 'a nice gesture if you were able to arrange a poem.'

And sure enough, an hour and a half before G.D.'s funeral, I received an e-mail from a journalist from *Het Laatste Nieuws*, asking whether a poet will be present, and if so, could the newspaper ask him a few questions beforehand. After a bitterly cold journey, I arrive at Schoonselhof Cemetery's funeral parlour at half past two, and a bit later the journalist arrives, notebook at the ready. He tells me that his modest neighbourhood investigation – the pharmacy, the neighbours, and the landlord – did not turn up much. Mr. G.D. does not appear to have any next of kin, no friends, no acquaintances. There was a second name, a 'Mr. Love', on his mailbox. The landlord confirms that for some time, a man by that name did live with Mr. G.D., but that he had departed some time ago. His name, in any case, has a promising ring.

The two pallbearers pull in and drive straight to the

scattering lawn, where they park. Then Bernard arrives. We'll wait for the newspaper photographer, who took a wrong turn into the cemetery's far entrance. Bernard asks how I'm doing, adding that he had a hard time writing his poem. I reply that it is a weird feeling to attend the funeral of a stranger on my birthday. I turn 25 today, celebrating a quarter of a century amongst the living. Fortunately I'm not really big on birthdays, especially on this particular day, at a cemetery where the iciness slices into your cheeks like a knife.

We walk over to the hearse with the curtained windows, and up races the photographer in his white car. At twenty past three it's time to begin the brief ceremony. We have given up on Mr. Love. We walk silently behind the hearse to the scattering lawn, fifteen metres ahead, while the photographer circles around Bernard, the pallbearer and me like a horsefly. The click of the camera continues unabated as we ascend the steps to the lawn. We stand in a semicircle around the urn, and Bernard offers a last word for Mr. G.D.

NO ONE

is the quiet one
whose existence was never confirmed
by anyone,

the one who left no trail,
who nobody visited
at home,

the invisible one,
who nobody saw
though he was looking at us,

the one nobody reckoned on,
who was never taken into account
as somebody who counted,

the speechless one
at the deaf walls
of next-door's racket,

the unfindable one
behind the blinds
this city closes,

the lifeless one
who only lives
for his rats,

a suspicion
we finally dispel
like a rumour,

a no one
who became someone
because he was no one.

Bernard Dewulf, translated by David Colmer

We pay our respects, one by one: Bernard, myself, and the journalist. Then the photographer, who had been doing his work from a distance, hustles over; he also wishes to pay his respects. The camera is no longer dangling around his neck. The urn is removed from the pedestal and the pallbearer carries it onto the lawn. 'Here?' he asks his colleague, once he reaches an empty spot in the grass. He scatters the ashes. There's not much: the skeleton has been reduced to rough granules.

The pallbearer invites me to lay the three purple roses I had brought with me near the ashes. As I walk onto the grass, I'm careful to watch my step. It is a grid with narrow, well worn paths – they're sometimes called 'elephant tracks'. We say our goodbyes and I tell them I'm going to raise a glass to the death of Mr. G.D., and to the twenty-five years I've been alive.

The next day there's an article in *Het Laatste Nieuws*. Aside from the headline – 'LONELY FAREWELL TO THE RAT MAN' – it is a good article, recalling, one last time, the life of Mr. G.D., paraphrasing Dewulf's poem: 'A nobody who became somebody because he was nobody.'

Mr. M. B.

Born Antwerp 30 September 1930, found dead
in his apartment 12 May 2013.
Ashes scattered 3 June 2013, Schoonselhof Cemetery
Duty poet: Andy Fierens

'At this point the pallbearer asks us to pay our last respects,' I say to Andy Fierens. We're standing side by side on the scattering lawn nearest the crematorium, but I can easily peer over the low hedges and see the other lawns. At the intersection of the four lawns, a few small palm trees rock gently in the wind. We make a quick bow.

We were late for Mr. M.B.'s funeral. When we reached the entrance to the crematorium – me running, Andy biking – the Firm's car was gone. The ashes had already been scattered. The death business waits for no one. Pallbearers are extremely punctual, poem or no poem.

I take my three white roses from the pedestal and stand on the cement border at the edge of the lawn. I see the coarse grey grains of ash settled in among the roots, and I lay the flowers with care in the grass.

I was on time at the wrong entrance to Schoonselhof Cemetery, and even spotted one of the partridges Etienne has mentioned before. It was a beautiful creature; I got as close as twenty metres, at which point it ran further away with every step I took, and finally flew off to a different hollow. When Andy arrived, we sat chatting on a bench in the sun, until I realized it was already three o'clock.

So now we have paid Mr. M.B. our last respects after all – Andy read out his poem for the grey flecks in the grass.

Where Mr. M.B.'s are actually scattered, we don't know.

I feel guilty about this stupid mistake, for the Firm, but mostly for Mr. M.B. Just as the silence at his funeral was deafening, during his life Mr. M.B. also had no one to talk to. Andy had visited his place of residence in Antwerp-South, and had spoken to a neighbour. She did not know Mr. M.B. – yes, they had exchanged a word or two in the corridor once, when there was something wrong with his television, and he asked if she could help. But it never went as far as sitting down together in front of their favourite soap.

'Eighty-three years old,' Andy adds. We walk back from the scattering lawn, glancing back just to be sure no one is there. No pallbearers or gravediggers. Nor did I hear from Renée. It was Cathy from the Firm who had e-mailed me Mr. M.B.'s information, as with the previous lonely funeral. Whether my contact with Renée has been broken for good, I don't know.

'Mr. M.B. had no one while he was alive, and even at his funeral, the poets show up late,' I say. This must never happen again, I promise myself.

* * *

the things a person touches
carry their imprint for a while
an existence leaves a trail
that slowly fades away

I don't know where I was when you –
I don't know where you were, only
that there was no one beside you
and hadn't been for years

like a satellite breaking free
of earth, that points its nose
at distant stars, lights up
for an instant then disappears
again in the immensity –
so is a human life

I don't know what I did that day
I don't know what you thought –
only that you were caught
in a net of echoes off the walls
and waited day after day
for someone to come for you

someone who would speak to you
in this life without a name

Andy Fierens, translated by David Colmer

Mrs. H. M.

*Born 1 July 1907 in Antwerp, died at Vinck Heymans
nursing home 20 August 2013.
23 August 2013, Schoonselfhof Cemetery
Duty poet: Lies Van Gasse*

Mrs. H.M. outlived everyone around her. She experienced two world wars, she married, lost her husband, moved into a room in an old-people's home, and died there at the age of one hundred and six. According to the staff at the nursing home, she had no children. Did she not want any, was she unable to have them, did she perhaps lose them? We do not know. The nurse with whom I speak on the telephone does tell me that Mrs. H.M. had a sister, who in 1991 joined her at the nursing home, but had passed away in the meantime. Mrs. H.M., however, had spent enough years at the home to be remembered: she enjoyed the occasional glass of champagne and liked the singer Louis Neefs. But whenever the staff put on a Louis Neefs record, she would turn her head away.

'Maybe the memories were too emotional,' said the nurse on the phone. 'She couldn't explain, because she'd lost her ability to speak.'

'She had a really long life.'

'A few months ago, when she turned 106, we threw her a big party. A couple of city officials even came to congratulate her.'

I go online in search of other Antwerp centenarians. It is not inconceivable that Mrs. H.M. belongs to an exclusive club of longevity record-holders. I learn that if you want to become the oldest documented Belgian, then your odometer has to read 111. In an old newspaper article I read that the oldest-ever Antwerpian blew out 107 candles, but has since died. I contact someone with an extensive archive, who can dig around to see if Mrs. H.M.'s respectable age won her any special accolades. It is a meagre consolation prize: you're a VIP at your 106th, but a nobody at your funeral.

In the end, *Het Laatste Nieuws* comes up with some more information. Mrs. H.M., it appears, was the third oldest Antwerpian. There is a 106-year-old, who is about to turn 107, but the current record-holder is already 107. No one in the metropolis beats this.

On the day of Mrs. H.M.'s cremation, there is a small item in the newspaper announcing her funeral, and that afternoon, two nursing home residents do make it, after all, assisted by a trio of aides, because the two ladies are no longer quite so mobile.

'I always set [sic] across from her at mealtimes,' says the one. 'It's my duty to attend her funeral, if she's got no children or anyone else. This way she can still go in company.' The other lady maintains that God was always with Mrs. H.M.: 'Our Hetty was never alone.' Hetty, that was Mrs. H.M.'s nickname.

Our modest procession follows the hearse to the second scattering garden down the lane. A camera team jogs along, so as to capture everything on film – today, Mrs. H.M. is newsworthy. At the scattering garden, there is no wheelchair ramp. The lady from the nursing home is prepared to observe the ritual from a distance, but I offer to carry her wheelchair up the steps. Halfway up she jokes: 'You're not gonna toss me in the oven too, heh?'

By the time everyone is in place, pallbearer Xavier has already placed the urn on the pedestal, and pallbearer Dennis speaks: 'We have gathered here together to return Mrs. H.M.'s earthly remains to nature. Each of us says goodbye as the heart tells us.' This is not the first time I've heard these phrases, but every time I'm struck by the way the words hit the nail on the head. You can do the craziest stunts or say the maddest things, as long it feels like the right way to say farewell. Now it is Lies Van Gasse's turn, with a text loosely based on Louis Neefs' 'Leave Us a Flower'. But she does not sing; she quietly reads out her poem.

* * *

This is a song for hair that's turned white,
for those who were born a lifetime ago.
This is a song for the voice of champagne,
for sisters who sing, for a desert of stone.

This is a song for your husband at home,
for dust on the roofs, as it came, as it passed.
You saw the streets, the cobbles were fading,
a year here in town was a balm to your heart.

This is a song for the soldiers who marched in,
for thundering sand, for the spray of the Scheldt.
Now that the memory itself has grown pale,
now certain to vanish like all that you felt.

Let's blow the dust
off the roofs, off the tiles.
Leave us a tree,
let us sing a duet.
Forget for a moment
how the moon shines on rooftops,
your language to us,
like a view of the sea.

You break and you hack and you drill through the hillsides
You make all those mountains of time stand in line.
Giants today look like midgets tomorrow.
Here there's no language, the moon sings like it's full.

Life's here today, but it's gone tomorrow,
for years it was hidden behind concrete walls.
We scatter it now in the glow of the lights,
nobody knows when you started to fall.

Lies Van Gasse, translated by David Colmer

Then Xavier scatters the ashes, and everyone can pay their last respects. The lady who does not require a wheelchair walks onto the lawn and gesticulates dramatically – 'Bye-bye,' she says, 'see you soon' – it is almost a rain dance. Or perhaps she is making a large cross; she is the one who believed God was at Mrs. H.M.'s side. With a small bow, I lay my three white roses in the grass next to the grey patch.

The nursing home residents are asked to say a few words about Hetty to the camera. Later tonight, the little we know about Mrs. H.M. will be repeated on the regional news. I express my sympathy with bearers Dennis and Xavier, with this heat, in their heavy, dark suits, and inquire whether they have many more services to see to.

'One more, and then it's weekend.'

'TGIF,' I say.

When I get home I discover two dead mice the cat has brought in. I carry them, wrapped in sheets of paper towel, to their final resting place in the trash can.

Mrs. N. D.

Born 4 August 1936 in Oostnieuwkerke,
died 27 October 2013 at Middelheim Hospital, Antwerp.
Tuesday 5 November 2013, Schoonselhof Cemetery
Duty poet: Max Temmerman

At Mrs. N.D.'s funeral the rain falls like a heavy horse blanket onto the ground, our heads, the coffin. That night it continues unabated; the next day, too, it pours stubbornly. It is a cold November rain that makes you want to stay indoors. But even though he's offered us a lift to the grave, I tell Etienne we'll walk behind the hearse. So I tread behind the rumbling vehicle, half under Max Temmerman's umbrella and half under Etienne's, the water dribbling down my cheeks.

'Maybe I should have picked a less exuberant model,' Max whispers. He glances upward at the brightly-coloured rainbow design of his umbrella. Etienne's is one size bigger, and jet-black. As we slowly walk onto the lane, we pass a group of cemetery regulars on a tour of historical graveyards. A few folks in wheelchairs, a couple of pushers, and a leader – in heavy jackets or plastic garbage bags – watch as we pass.

Behind us is a car with a man and a woman in it. Neighbours of Mrs. N.D. who I had met that morning. I'm glad they didn't let the rain put them off. Mrs. N.D. lived outside the Antwerp Ring, in what is still part of Borgerhout, right near Te Boelaar Park. I saw a school and the Flanders Hydraulics Research lab. A lively neighbourhood.

When I rang a random doorbell, a window on the second floor opened and a woman's head stuck out over the sill.

She had visitors, she said, and knew nothing about Mrs. N.D. Said I should try higher up, fifth floor: that neighbour did her shopping. There were only six doorbells and six letter slots, but none bore Mrs. N.D.'s name. The next-door neighbour's was there, though. She too stuck her head out the window and I shouted up to her over the traffic noise.

I learned that they had an warm friendship, she and Mrs. N.D. They only had to cross the hallway, through just two doors. Did their shopping together, told stories, shared their lives. Her mouth purses shut when I tell her what we'll do at the funeral: bid her farewell with the words of a poet. She nods in acknowledgement; there's not much more to say.

I heard from the Firm that there are two sisters as well. One with whom there has been no contact for some years, and another who is senile and confined to an old-people's home in Wingene. They will not attend. The funeral will be an intimate affair consisting of the pallbearers, Max, myself, and the grieving couple from next door.

The hearse in front of us comes to a halt, and the car with the neighbours pulls onto the shoulder. I do not look back, but think of Max's words after he had gone for a walk in Mrs. N.D.'s neighbourhood earlier this week: 'It's chic and expensive and tidy. Posters taped to the inside of windows, ornamental gourds on windowsills, and welcoming benches out front. The kind of neighbourhood that calls itself a "meeting place"… and still, a neighbourhood with lonely people.'

When the coffin is slid out of the hearse, the neighbour gets choked up. She cries, says she can't handle it. She cannot walk onto the soggy lawn, she won't do it. Her husband grasps her hand, and Etienne gives an encouraging nod. Everyone, including the sister who would not come, should have seen how Etienne took the neighbour lady's bouquet and my three white roses and, in the pouring rain, lays them on the wet coffin lid, and informs the meagre company that, with a few words from the poet, we will now say farewell to a shared a life.

AS PER USUAL

This morning I walked past the building
you called home. Sunlight angling through the trees,
approach roads slicing through the city
like hot knives. I know it's hard to tell,
but not much seems to have changed since you –

I saw a man being towed along
by a cross-eyed dog. A tiny boy
blocked the pavement with a fort
he'd made of skipping rope, a football
and a bike. Nobody could get by
but everyone just seemed to laugh it off.

The door to Taverne Erasmus was open wide.
A skinny woman scrubbed the floor and sent
a cascade of suds and congealed chat
across the blue stone to my feet.

In a creeper on a fence I heard
three transistor radios that sounded
like out-of-tune pigeons. Further away
the Ring was humming and up in the sky
planes were descending,
ready to land.

Everything as per usual. When little things change,
for instance, age, they're only the slightest accents
in an ongoing text whose essence
remains unchanged.

This time it's you. The one who's gone away.
We take our hats in our hands.
And say a last farewell.

Max Temmerman, translated by David Colmer

The neighbour and her husband stand close to Max, under his rainbow umbrella, to hear what words still need to be spoken for Mrs. N.D. When he's finished, Max folds up the wet sheet of paper and hands it to the neighbour, who nods appreciatively. Nothing more will be said today. Then comes the bowing at the coffin. The neighbour and her husband walk hand in hand away from the grave, but I remain, I want to see Mrs. N.D. lowered into the dark, waterlogged ground.

Mr. B. M.

Born on 28 June 1953 in Temse,
died in Stuivenberg Hospital in Antwerp 1 November 2013.
Tuesday 12 November 2013, Schoonselhof Cemetery
Duty poet: Peter Theunynck

The deceased's sister and I have one mutual friend on Facebook. Her profile photo is a haunted house engulfed in a swarm of bats. In the past she also used a picture of her dog and a picture of her canary. She plays Pet Rescue Saga, Farm Heroes Saga, and Smoothie Swipe. With only a few clicks of the mouse I know far more about Mr. B.M.'s sister than about Mr. B.M. himself. He was not on Facebook.

The six degrees of separation theory postulates that any two random people on Earth can be connected to each other via just five other people. I was separated from Mr. B.M. by only three degrees. But I will never meet him; Mr. B.M. died on the first of November, All Saints' Day, in his social-housing flat behind the Permeke library in Antwerp city centre. He will receive a lonely funeral. His sister does not wish to be contacted about the funeral. On Facebook, she likes 'Verses, Values, Viewpoints', so I assume she'll also be pleased that a poet will say something at her brother's burial.

What went wrong between brother and sister, I don't need to know. What is clear, however, is that Mr. B.M., aside from our three degrees of separation, did not really have much connection with those around him. I went to his social-housing apartment building, a grey cement block behind the library, and rang a few doorbells. One person answered, but informed me through the crackly intercom that she knew nothing about her neighbour.

I return a few days later: being the weekend, there are now more people at home. One does not wish to speak to me, another says he'll come downstairs.

'Yeah, he's dead. D'you know when they're gonna come pick up his stuff? Everything's still in his apartment!' The neighbour does not smell so nice, the odour of someone who hasn't had a wash for a while; I take a step back, and he moves a little closer again. One of his eyes is misaligned, it is turned off to one side, so he probably doesn't see me very well. I ask if he knew Mr. B.M.

'No, no. Last week they came to tell me he was dead. I dunno any more than that. His stuff's still in there.' I don't know about Mr. B.M.'s belongings – his easy chair, table, chairs, television – or what will happen to them. He had been married, and then divorced. Did not produce any children.

On Tuesday there is an unrelenting drizzle. It has been raining nonstop for a week now; the rain started the day Mr. B.M. died and will only let up the day after his funeral. As I enter the cemetery carrying three white roses, I see that Peter Theunynck has taken shelter under the eaves of the guardhouse. A hearse from the Firm is idling at the beginning of the lane, with pallbearers Xavier and Etienne in the front seat.

'We needn't wait,' Etienne says, ten minutes before schedule, and the three of us walk behind the hearse to the grave. There is a long silence before Etienne speaks again. 'The director of the cemetery's coming too. And do you see that woman with the umbrella? She's an inspector. So everything had better go smoothly.'

'We'll follow your lead, as usual,' I reassure him. 'It's Peter's first time as duty poet.'

'Can't you do it, then? You're experienced. And maybe two poems instead of just one?'

I can't tell if Etienne is kidding or not. I tell him I've got complete faith in Peter Theunynck – he'll be excellent, addressing Mr. B.M. for the last time. And indeed he is. Mr. B.M.'s lonely funeral goes off without a hitch.

GOODBYE, B. M.

You lived a stone's throw from the library,
but your story's not in any books.

No neighbours who recall your name. Only an entry
in the registry confirms your existence.

Your mother's waters broke on the bridge at Temse.
A male nurse closed your eyes in Stuivenberg.

And in between, a lot of white, like the space
between the lines of a poem or like the tundra in winter:

the snow has erased all traces.
How quiet it can be beneath this hood of feathers.

When it thaws, all kinds of things will surface:
a passport, a school report, perhaps a bike,

the photo of the woman you once left,
your pocket knife, your sunglasses, your insurance card.

You came into the world on a Sunday, almost summer.
Not a cloud in the sky. A gentle breeze was blowing.

By the Scheldt, in the reeds, couples were kissing.
Vera Lynn was singing 'We'll meet again' on the radio.

Not a lot of sun and kisses were in store for you.
And nobody longed to meet you again.

On 1 November you made your quiet departure.
By now you must have got quite far.

Maybe there you'll start to feel at home. Maybe
there you'll build a dauntless new beginning.

Peter Theunynck, translated by David Colmer

We bow in order: Etienne first, then the director of the cemetery, the woman inspector, Peter and myself. Once the coffin has been lowered, the pallbearers leave the area, slap the wood dust from their shoulders, and drive away. We tarry at the grave, mutedly discussing what we have just seen, until the excavator comes rolling over the cement pavement to fill the pit with dirt.

The director offers us coffee in the 'Castle' on the cemetery grounds, and tells us about the planned renovations to the building, to be precise, the restoration of the nineteenth-century ceiling decoration introduced by the then-lady of the house. We gaze upward at paintings of monkeys, birds, dogs, and the hunt.

'More coffee, anyone?' the director asks.

Mr. F. V. G.

Born 10 February 1935 in Antwerp,
died in his apartment 5 December 2013.
Thursday, 19 December 2013, Schoonselhof Cemetery
Duty poet: Joke van Leeuwen

Mr. F.V.G. lived above a coach trimmer. I had never heard that term before: 'coach trimmer', otherwise known as an automotive upholsterer. On the ground floor is a large white drive-in car-port; upstairs, two flats. The eighty-year-old coach trimmer is also the landlord, and answers the door to fill me in on the unknown life of Mr. F.V.G.

'I found him. It's like this. My son, he works here too, noticed that F.'s mailbox was overflowing. So I went up and knocked on the door. And not lightly either, y'know? Not that I meant to bash a hole in the door, but they could hear it all the way out on the street. There was no answer, so I called the police.

'I have a key, so I was the first one inside, but the cops told me to stay in the hallway. But I'd already got a glimpse of him. He was lying on the floor, next to the table with the computer. You know just how it went: he was sitting at the computer, and fell over sideways. Dead.'

The landlord performs his version of Mr. F.V.G.'s death for me, in the doorway of his house. He lets his torso flop all the way over to one side, and says 'boom'. His sky-blue eyes are glassy in his crinkled face.

'Suffocated. He smoked himself to death. For years I've been telling him: That don't sound good. All that coughing. A while ago I replaced all the windows. As a souvenir I kept an old piece of window frame in the garage – the nicotine's

146

practically dripping off it! At the end he could hardly even make it up the stairs.'

'Did he do his own shopping? Or did he have help from someone?'

'Sometimes I saw him carrying bags of groceries. See that little green car across the street? Once a month he would drive it to Hulst, just across the border. Stuff's cheaper in Holland. I says to him, F., I says, why do you drive all the way to Hulst and back? At your age?

'Other than that we didn't have much contact. He lived upstairs, but was, you know, reclusive. But as a tenant: A-OK. The rent was always in my bank account before the first of the month. Very prompt, that man. But never a visitor. In the twenty, thirty years he lived there I never saw anyone at his door. He once mentioned having a sister, but she died before he did.'

'Do you know what he did for a living?'

'Started as a street sweeper in Antwerp. Then he got promoted, got to drive a delivery van around town. For the 'lectricity fellows. That was better work, and he preferred it too, driving around in a van.' After this, the coach trimmer wants to show me his upholstery shop, where his son is at work. 'This is my life,' he says. 'I still work here too, but no set hours. It's my playground.'

I stick my head through the open door of the garage and say goodbye to Mr. F.V.G.'s ex-landlord.

Pallbearer Xavier is under doctor's orders to quit smoking, and pallbearer Dennis tells us about the throngs of Christmas shoppers in the city centre.

'For the vocal cords. Quit smoking, for the vocal cords.'

'Doctors always tell you to quit smoking. Even if there's nothing wrong with you.'

'Nice floral arrangement you've got there.'

That's right. While I normally bring three white roses for the unfortunate departed, now I have a extra large bouquet. There are even a few green palm leaves sticking out.

'We had a donation, for flowers.' Last week I received

a card from an older lady, in old-fashioned handwriting, addressed 'to the poet'. In shaky letters, it read: 'I have read, with great pleasure, all about your project. Here is a modest contribution for a cup of coffee and a bouquet of flowers.' Today, I can splurge a bit.

We chat for the rest of the fifteen-minute wait, alongside the hearse with Mr. F.V.G. inside. Joke van Leeuwen joins us, and we decide to get the show on the road. Dennis drives the hearse, and Joke, Xavier and I follow. The mood in our small group is relaxed, so relaxed that we've reached Section W1 before we know it, and Xavier gives us the signal to stop. We need to make room for the coffin and the formation of five pallbearers.

FOR F. V. G.

See those whose job is tending to the streets,
who sweep away the daily grime and keep
the lamps alight. See them in their darkness,
homeward bound.

Greet this man who was. Bow for the silence
of his life. Respect these joints grown stiff from labour.
Look back to see another gate that no one opens.
Honour him with this cold,

gleaming, glassy, wind-blown
and belated ode.

Joke van Leeuwen, translation by David Colmer

148

Joke recites in a full voice. The five pallbearers stand in a semicircle around Mr. F.V.G., then disperse in order to pull the nylon straps under the coffin, and lower the rocking boat into the grave. When Mr. F.V.G.'s coffin comes to rest, we wish each other well in these last few days of the old year, five days before Christmas. Some of us will go away for the holidays. Keep your head warm, take good care of your loved ones, there's a new beginning around the corner.

Jayson N.

Born in Paris 9 December 2013,
died Edegem Hospital 22 January 2014.
6 March 2014, Schoonselhof Cemetery
Duty poet: Maarten Inghels

The officiant takes the small coffin containing the baby in his arms, puts his left foot in front of his right, then his right foot in front of his left, steps with deliberate tread onto the border of the children's cemetery. I follow him, three white roses in my hands; then come Gilles and Martin from the Schoonselhof administrative office, two of their female colleagues who have been rustled up at the last minute – I don't yet know their names – and lastly, the second pallbearer, who stays behind to shut the tailgate of the oversized rear deck of the hearse. The officiant carefully places the coffin on the ground beside the freshly-dug pit, a narrow, dark shaft in the lawn, after which we form a semicircle around it. Around us, the other patches of overturned soil in this specially-designated section are easy to count. They are molehills: graves of a foetus, an infant, a pint-sized person.

Just now a Muslim ceremony took place here, with four adults and an imam in attendance. We watched from the drive how the imam held forth and gesticulated. Their ritual was elaborate and extensive. From the gravedigger, leaning on his spade next to us, we learned that this was the parents' second dead child. Afterwards, the imam came over to offer his condolences, and inquired who the parents were. We stammered a bit; Gilles was hastily designated as interim father. The five of us have gathered here for the funeral of a child, a baby in fact, until very recently unknown to us.

Born in Paris 9 December last year, left for dead at Edegem Hospital on 22 January. Lived for twenty-two days in 2013, and twenty-two days in 2014 – all told, hardly forty-four days old.

'The parents showed up at the hospital in Liège and left behind a dubious address in Italy,' says Vicky, of the Firm, over the telephone. 'But the infant eventually died of neglect, in Edegem's university medical centre. No sign of the parents.' The mother is said to be Serbian, the father Romanian – but you can never be sure, not in this haphazard odyssey along cities and countries.

Did they lack the money for decent care and food? Was the child already sick at birth? There is also some uncertainty as to the baby boy's name, Jayson. Two civil registry numbers were discovered, each with a different name – or is it a matter of two babies born on the same day? I phone a poet whose life is a whirlwind of children, family bliss, 'little days', but it is vacation; he is off somewhere with the kids. With less than twenty-four hours left before the funeral, I start writing a poem myself. By evening, it is finished, save a single comma.

On the morning of the funeral I receive an e-mail with some last-minute details. It seems that the parents – and by extension, their infant son – were in Belgium illegally. This is something that is apparently noted at birth. They surfaced from nowhere, and to nowhere little Jayson shall now go.

Officiant Rick, who has laid the small coffin next to the pit, signals that it is time for the final words. In the five years that I have attended lonely funerals, this is the first child we will bury, and on that 6 March, amongst the molehills, next to a coffin barely an arm's length long, I hope with all my heart that this abandoned Jayson will be the last. I take a step closer and clear my throat.

YOUR ROUND-THE-WORLD TRIP IN FORTY-FOUR DAYS

Your round-the-world trip in forty-four days:
Romania, Serbia, Italy, Paris, Liège, Edegem,
Wilrijk, Antwerp, small white coffin, nothingness.

And this while, by and large, a longer life
fits between cradle and grave. You grow up,
deserve to fall in love on a Barcelona beach,

discover Norway's northern lights,
have a child, or two, or three, to whom
you'll sing lullabies – and only then see Naples.

Not this. We'd hoped to ask you
about your two names, the scent of all those cities
in your blood, the start and end of an alphabet.

Not this: still toothless, and already Europe's lost son,
with your unnamed passport and faulty compass,
and two parents' addressless regret.

Maarten Inghels, translated by Jonathan Reeder

    I take a step back and watch as the coffin is brought above the grave cut. But the size is not right. Little Jayson is too big for the hole in the ground. The grave-digger sets the coffin off to one side, his glance asks Rick whether we want to excuse ourselves, but no, we will wait here for what has to happen. The spade goes back into the ground, trimming off some five more centimetres of earth on three sides of the cut, about half a meter deep. The work is executed thoroughly; the digger stabs sharply into the lawn, the metal blade sounds hard as it slices into the ground, followed by the dull thud of shovelled earth.

With this funeral, everything that happens is in miniature. No nylon straps, no team of pallbearers, no backhoe to refill the grave. The officiant lowers the coffin from under his armpit, lays the folded sheet of paper with the poem on the lid, scatters dirt over the wood, like a blanket. Then a small hillock takes shape, a swell in the landscape, that the digger painstakingly presses, with the back of his spade, into a six-sided oblong form, a sand castle for Jayson into which, lastly, the white roses are stuck: medals for a tiny castaway.

Mr. R. H.

Born 13 November 1947 in Wilrijk, died 28 March 2014.
11 April 2014, Schoonselhof Cemetery
Duty poet: Lies Van Gasse

It's always a surprise to stumble over a bit of the lonely dead's past on Google. Usually the only hits turn up a genealogy website with namesakes from another century, but with Mr. R.H., I hit the jackpot. All three top-ranked hits link me to cycling websites, whose archives brim with records of amateur as well as professional cyclists. Mr. R.H. was a cyclist of note for one single race. Or, to put it better, in one single race he ended in the top three, earning himself a place for eternity in the annals of competitive cycling.

1966. Second place in National Championship, Track, Tandem, Amateurs, Belgium, Rocourt (Liège), Belgium.

There is a little Belgian flag next to the entry, to give the country for which he achieved this honour some extra cachet. I had never heard of tandem track racing, but there are plenty of videos to be found on YouTube. The cyclists sit on a single bike, and ride in circles around an indoor track.

Mr. R.H. was nineteen when he shared a racing tandem – up front or at the rear, we don't know – and came in second in the national indoor track tandem cycling championships in Liège. His co-rider, Mr. J.P., can also be found in the cycling archives. Second place in the national amateur tandem championships was likewise Mr. J.P.'s sole claim to cycling fame. Did those two young men ever mount a cycle again after that, did they train on the streets of Wilrijk, two boys on a single racing bike, preparing for another national championship? Did they stay in touch in the years that followed?

Who got to keep the trophy? Did they each get one? Or was it a 'rolling trophy'?

Mr. R.H.'s address offers no answers either. He lived in one of the three high-rise blocks of flats overlooking Kiel Park. Standing at the mailboxes under the building's hundreds of windows, it was impossible to deduce from his house number which floor he lived on, and which number belonged to his neighbours. There was no one I could speak to.

Nor is there much in the dossier that Social Services had drawn up on Mr. R.H. He was entitled to cleaning help and home care, but had not been on Social Services' watch since 2002. In the dossier's reports, he is described as a loner with a complex range of health issues. He had apparently traded tandem cycling for a solitary sickbed.

Mr. R.H. is scattered on Friday, under a feeble spring sun. Poet Lies Van Gasse texted me the night before the funeral that her poem was 'an ode to track cycling'. The Firm's hearse drives up at two minutes to twelve; five minutes later we're at the scattering lawn. Lies reads out her poem; with a few swings, Mr. R.H. is scattered, after which we pay our last respects to the patch of ash in the grass. I lay my three white roses at the feet that will never again pedal a racing bike.

FOR R. H.

You've just turned twenty:
smooth legs, polished parquet,
accelerating circles, two by two.

Your life is a game of kilometres,
synchronised rhythms of four legs.
Your tread, but also your body rises

and then the years, white with dust,
burying your avalanche of circuits.
You are left grey in a house
and gently close your eyes.

The floor of your room tilts and turns.
Loud light blacks out the windows.

A barking dog spins in your bike,
but you are tender.

Lies Van Gasse, translated by David Colmer

Mr. A. D.

*Born 18 April 1920 in Wilrijk, died 18 April 2014 at
Lozanahof nursing home in Antwerp.
Monday 28 April 2014, Schoonselhof Cemetery
Duty poet: Joke van Leeuwen*

Dying on one's birthday: that is a sign of either patient planning or sheer coincidence. Mr. A.D. died on his ninety-fourth birthday in his bed at the nursing home. Whether he blew out the candles on his cake first, I do not know.

The Social Services' dossier on Mr. A.D. shows that he used live on his own, in a high-rise at the edge of Antwerp-South, until he moved to an assisted-living facility. There he was still relatively independent; the home care people would drop by for the shopping and household help, but dementia eventually caught up with him, so in 2006 he was transferred to a nursing home.

A staff member from Social Services told me there was a nephew and his wife, but they hadn't been to visit for years. 'Their contact information is no longer up to date. I wrote to inform them, but I don't know if they'll respond.' They will not respond.

The staff at the nursing home do return my phone call. Having left my name and number, I am called back within the hour by the nurse who knew Mr. A.D. the longest and the best.

'He was a calm and easygoing person,' she says. 'Back in 2006 he walked in here on his own, but at the end was confined to a wheelchair. He had cataracts, too, so his vision was impaired.'

'Do you know what he did for a living? Or if he had

any hobbies?'

'Ah, he was a baseball fan, and had played it in his youth. Whenever we steered the conversation in that direction, he perked right up.'

Mr. A.D.'s wife had apparently passed away some time ago. All he possessed were the thoughts of his wife, of baseball, and of birthdays.

But this seems to be enough for duty poet Joke van Leeuwen. The next day she e-mails me a vintage photograph picturing a group of baseball players assembled in front of a net, their bats fanned out on the grass in front of them, and at the lower left, a few small boys. It's from an international reference book about baseball, available for online perusal.

She found it by googling Mr. A.D.'s name along with the word 'baseball'. According to the caption, Mr. A.D. is the 'boy, 2nd from left'. The photograph is dated 1930, when Mr. A.D. was ten years old. The caption continues: 'Local baseball players took on Japanese sailors in the early days of the sport in Belgium.'

The book explains that in the early twentieth century, Japanese sailors spent their free time in Antwerp playing baseball. Their diamond was the Wilrijkseplein, where youths like Mr. A.D. would hang around and learn the sport. Teams were formed: the Antwerp Cats, Belteco Baseball Club, and General Motors.

Baseball was, in 1930, new to Belgian sports, and Mr. A.D. was a keen player. He is pictured with a dark American-style cap pulled in a butch manner over his eyes, 'Terukun' pinned to his jersey – the name of the Japanese team. Others wear sailors' caps.

The frogs in the canal croak loudly as I sit on the bench in front of the crematorium, waiting for Joke and the pallbearers. Joke's compact car pulls up first, and then pallbearer Rick suddenly appears out of nowhere.

'We're ready,' he says.

The hearse carrying Mr. A.D. drives ahead, and we follow. On the way to the scattering lawn, we pass small groups of mourners here and there who bow their heads as we pass; soft whispers.

FOR A. D., FORMER BASEBALL PLAYER

Being able to win, yes, a home run
now and then, losing that, vision clouded,
joints stiff, the wife already gone. How
much present was left in your head?

The knowledge of. Of heavy hitting,
of speed, of keen eyes, of winning.
And that it all would have to pass,
but once was there, as your beginning.

Joke van Leeuwen, translated by David Colmer

When the poem is finished, I'm still holding my three white roses. Rick gives a sign that I can place them near the grey square in the grass. I hesitate, because Mr. A.S. is lying some seven meters from the edge of the scattering lawn. To get there, I'll have to walk across other grey patches in the grass.

My roses lie in the field. One last home run.

On the way back to the city, the sky is grey, it is tainted air, the tension of an impending storm. I think: come, rain, rinse the ash from my shoes.

Mr. A. B.

Born 12 October 1934 in Antwerp,
died at St. Anna nursing home 8 July 2014.
Thursday, 17 July 2014, Schoonselhof Cemetery
Duty poet: Max Temmerman

According to the staff of the nursing home, Mr. A.B. was a real jokester, and went through life laughing out loud. He loved women, and smoked a lot. Laughter, ladies, cigarettes. Those three words summed up Mr. A.B.'s life. His profession is not known, nor are his hobbies. To be summed up in three words after one's death – the simplicity of 79 years of life.

HEROIC FEATS

Everyone can lead a great and thrilling life,
though some make their heroic feats
depend on daunting preconditions.

They require monstrous foes or civilisations
they can fight at the far end of the world.

Years later they return in triumph with tales so tall
no one will ever know the truth.

Others spend their lives on one square inch.
They never move, they have no need
of pricy props. Their memory gives depth

to a map of houses, shops and streets.
They live like sleepwalkers in the dark:
more slowly, yes, but with more caution too. These heroes

add a new dimension to our too hurried lives.
An apt example of one such feat? They say
you had the brightest smile in the street.

Max Temmerman, translated by David Colmer

Mr. P. B. D.

Born 12 August 1925 in Bergen op Zoom (Netherlands),
died at home in Merksem 19 December 2014.
Monday, 5 January 2015, Schoonselhof Cemetery
Duty poet: Bernard Dewulf

The cleaning lady had called police. She had rung the doorbell and no one answered, or else she had a key and saw Mr. P.B.D. sitting in his favourite chair. How many dead clients, in the course her life, had the cleaning lady found at work?

Mr. P.B.D. was an 89-year-old Dutch man with a daughter, but the search for his child has so far turned up nothing. So fourteen days after Mr. P.B.D. was found, Social Services decides to give him a lonely funeral. For 'an ordinary man', as Bernard Dewulf says in his poem.

* * *

Presumably you were what's known
as an ordinary man, all tracks erased
before he's swallowed by the grass.

But maybe we should ask
the grass itself

how great you might have been,
singing, staring, shuffling
and every day a star in your dressing gown,

shining bright

in silent rooms where the grass has started sprouting,
as fierce and unheard
as only an ordinary man can be.

Bernard Dewulf, translated by David Colmer

POSTSCRIPT

Over the course of six years, 85 ordinary people got a poem at their funeral, whether they wanted it or not.[7] Regardless of their religion, place of birth, or whether they spoke the language of the poem.

Anyone who has ever visited a 'potter's field' knows what cheerlessness is. Simple wooden markers, no more than that, indicate the place where someone is buried. Temporary reminders, until a proper tombstone is placed, but just as often, this is as far as it goes. They point upwards like arrows. The deceased's name and year of death are chalked on in white. No date of birth. Here, one's age is irrelevant. On most of them it's just a patch of grass, but here and there one encounters a proper headstone, if the family found a sock under the bed to pay for a granite memorial. If no one visits the grave, time will wear away the name, and the wooden marker will splinter and tip over onto the grass, after which the municipality will clear it away. Nothing will remind the visitor that there is a grave, that someone is resting there in peace.

In Antwerp, a lonely funeral takes twelve minutes. In Amsterdam, attendees first gather in a chapel, play three pieces of recorded music, the poet recites his poem, after which they head out to the grave. I was present at most of the Antwerp funerals, I wrote a report afterwards, I was engaged, gave interviews with the other poets for radio, television, newspapers. Those 'ordinary' people have, these last few years, received an extraordinary amount of attention from the general public, raising the inevitable question of what impression these dead-ordinary folks left on the poet.

Like a journalist from a regional newspaper, I delve into these people's ordinary lives until the poet has enough

[7] At the time of this translation, the counter in Antwerp reached 112, and in Amsterdam 222.

material to compose a poem. I am a detective who traipses through Antwerp in search of their sealed-up apartments, houses, social-welfare flats. The name on the doorbell plate is worn, but with a little luck it will reveal a brief story about a former profession, an unusual hobby, a friendship with the neighbour. The more I learn, the deeper it affects me.

People sometimes suspect me of morbid fascination, as though I sit home polishing skulls, and are surprised when I show up wearing something more colourful than black. And they wonder why, at such a young age, I spend so much time in cemeteries. But the 'lonely funeral' has less to do with death than with the lives of a hundred or so city dwellers. Funeral undertakers not only tend the deceased, but the survivors too. They satisfy their most bizarre wishes, or assuage their deepest emotions with a ritual. And language always plays a key role in that grieving process. Those left behind search for the words to describe what has happened. We need language to make sense of something we don't understand, something beyond our spiritual comprehension. I am convinced that poetry is the most suitable instrument for this task.

Poems tell us just as much about how we should deal with life as with death, or else they admit that we've got no clue, that we are simply unable to cope with death's profound unknown. In attempting to sketch a correct and complete portrait of the deceased, we fail more often than we succeed. In most cases we sum up the death and the life of the stranger in a few words, a fine-tuned poem: silent, household help, alone.

Our subjects lived in this city like phantoms. Often, they leave no trace behind. This book is a collection of their forgotten lives, of the quest for the right words. A brief funeral with a few soothing words at the grave might not make much of a difference, but it is an attempt, based on the conviction that everyone deserves the respect to be seen. In life, and in death.

Maarten Inghels

165